On Love and Friendship
in the Indian Context and Sigmund Freud

On Love and Friendship
in the Indian Context and Sigmund Freud

Manashi Dasgupta

Edited by
Probal Dasgupta

Indian Council of Philosophical Research
New Delhi

DK PRINTWORLD
Publishers of Indian Traditions

Cataloging in Publication Data — DK
[Courtesy: D.K. Agencies (P) Ltd. <docinfo@dkagencies.com>]

Dasgupta, Manashi, 1928-2010, **author.**
On love and friendship in the Indian context
and Sigmund Freud / Manashi Dasgupta ;
edited by Probal Dasgupta.
pages cm
Includes bibliographical references.
ISBN 13: 9788124608227

1. Love – India. 2. Friendship – India. 3. Psychology and philosophy – India. 4. Philosophy, Indic. 5. Freud, Sigmund, 1856-1939. I. Dasgupta, Probal, 1953-, editor. II. Indian Council of Philosophical Research, issuing body. III. Title.

DDC 150.1 23

ISBN 13: 978-81-246-0822-7
First published in India, 2015 Print run : 550 copies

Published by:
INDIAN COUNCIL OF PHILOSOPHICAL RESEARCH
Darshan Bhawan, 36 Tughlakabad Institutional Area
Mehrauli–Badarpur Road, New Delhi - 110 062

and

D.K. PRINTWORLD (P) LTD.
Regd. Office: Vedaśrī, F-395, Sudarshan Park
(Metro Station: Ramesh Nagar), New Delhi – 110 015
Phones: (011) 2545 3975, 2546 6019; *Fax*: (011) 2546 5926
e-mail: indology@dkprintworld.com
Website: www.dkprintworld.com

Printed by : D.K. Printworld (P) Ltd. New Delhi

To
the friends

who co-organized with her
the Tagore Centenary Celebrations
on the Cornell University Campus
in 1961

Editor's Preface

THIS monograph was submitted to the Indian Council of Philosophical Research (ICPR) in 1988 as a project report (for Project No. F.1-18/86 [P&R]) by my mother Manashi Dasgupta (1928–2010). Her approach, combining philosophy with psychology, is articulated more clearly in this text than in the writings published during her lifetime. I am indebted to ICPR for arranging for its posthumous publication. ICPR is not responsible for the delay; I am; and I personally thank Amita Chatterjee, Nirmalya Narayan Chakraborty, Saroj Kanta Kar, Michael McGhee, Mrinal Miri, Arun Misra, Mohan Ramanan, Manendra Pratap Singh, M. Sridhar and P.S. Sundaram for several good turns that helped turn the manuscript into this book that you see.

The following sentence from Chapter 3 of this monograph succinctly articulates the priorities motivating the inquiry reported here: "Chitrangada is a celebration of joyful womanly love blended with personal accountability and self-respect". I hope readers will find the following exposition faithful to those priorities. My purpose in this preface is to suggest that this text is best read as an essay on the constitutive role of friendship and other interpersonal ties as factors contributing to the environment required for serious and equitable discussion between accountable adults to take place. Only if such discussions in micro-social milieux flourish can macro-societal democratic processes come into their own. The reception of this text will take place under contradictory pressures exerted by the global pre-context in which it was incubated and the global post-context of its use by readers today. Other factors become visible when we look at the milieu of intellectual production from which this monograph draws its coordinates. The triangle that this preface highlights – pre-context, post-context, milieu of formulation – may prove methodologically useful as a way of approaching other texts as well.

In its terms of reference this text takes for granted a world whose institutions were based on the ways of warfare. In Manashi Dasgupta's childhood, the world was frankly divided into imperially controlled segments. Neither the geopolitical managers of such control nor their intellectuals were apologetic about the conceptual presuppositions of the world order of colonial Herrenvölker. That order, they argued, was based on a "realism" rooted in a "scientific" understanding of the place of humans vis-à-vis the natural universe and vis-à-vis each other's "hard-headed" pursuit of cultural, economic and political self-interest. In that world, thanks to efforts by the victorious allies in the Second World War to safeguard "freedom" and "liberal democracy" against "racism" and "fascism", the victors did not find it ironic that most societies expected to be under authoritarian rule for the foreseeable future – openly assuming that the Hobbesian war of all against all was here to stay – and that "tender-minded" friendship was thus seen as on the whole a way to escape the worst consequences of the ubiquity of such regimes.

Under the shadow of the war of all against all, your enemy's enemies were your friends, especially if circumstances happened to throw you together and make coalition building look like a plausible move to make. Friendship was a strategy. In such an order of things only an unrealistic dissident, who not only rejected the premises that were in place but was proposing a full-blown alternative of her own "with a little help from [her] friends", would find it meaningful to offer a serious characterization of friendship that did not reduce it to a sublimation of love, to explore the self-understanding of friends present and past, or to bring such a conceptualization face to face with other serious formulations available.

But we are reading this document in a very different world, are we not, one in which formal democracy with formal freedom of the press appears to have become the prevalent norm. These circumstances should have enabled citizens and their states to build institutions that take peace as their point of reference. But such a process has not exactly taken off. Proponents of serious friendship still find themselves marginalized as toothless utopia-mongers. The theories of the "real world" that remain in place (with aggression-laden preferences surfacing in the use of *toothless* as a term of censure) refuse to conceptualize the third value, fraternity, on the same footing as liberty and equality. And yet conversations between friends are where the public discourse is incubated. The theoreticians' resolute and unembarrassed neglect of friendship, pushing its actual role into inappropriately marginal niches in our account of how society works and in proposals about where we should be headed, has catastrophically undermined substantive thinking on the place of the consultative ethos in democratic processes.

Manashi Dasgupta's monograph on friendship and its associates articulates a response to this predicament that goes back to the practices that she and her husband Arun Kumar Dasgupta pioneered in the early 1950s. They were committed to ensuring that children from poor families in the neighbourhood received loosely structured instruction in literacy and numeracy skills and ran a wall newspaper called *Spandan,* "(heart) beat, pulsation"; but this was not all. The *Spandan* circle led by this couple anchored itself in a loose congregation of friends rather than relatives – friends who took open and relaxed conversation seriously. The (adult) friends who made the *Spandan* enterprise then and later a vibrant site of companionship and discourse included individuals who were to become celebrities in the Anglophone academic world, such as Jitendra Nath Mohanty, Ashin Das Gupta and Tapan Raychaudhuri. The philosopher Mohanty and the historian Raychaudhuri have documented their debt to this enterprise (Mohanty, *Between Two Worlds: East and West*, Delhi: Oxford University Press, 2002; Raychaudhuri, *Bangalnama*, Kolkata: Ananda, 2007). But the *Spandan* circle was no mere academic salon. The incubation that took place there drew on the moral, intellectual and aesthetic resources of the resurgence that made South Asia in the 1950s a beacon of hope.

Of course, the resources that nourished the *Spandan* circle were also available to their peers; but this circle, and its continuations in the 1960s and later, added value by using them as a basis for launching what participants later came to see as an innovative enterprise. After the Dasguptas' passing, friends of theirs such as Mohanty, Raychaudhuri and Asok Sen emphasized how important it was for them to have been initiated into the art of forming and sustaining durable bonds of friendly dialogue across political and aesthetic differences that kept in view the importance of democratic processes in one's private lives. Mohanty and Raychaudhuri have documented their experiences, as mentioned above. Sen, who stayed on in Kolkata, actively continued the intellectual exchange. He provided feedback on the draft of Manashi's 1977 monograph on social psychology and the Indian milieu (*Samaj-Mon*, "Society and Mind", Firma K.L. Mukhopadhyay, Kolkata). Later, as the editor of *Baromas*, Sen published articles by Manashi that led to her 1987 psychological study of Rabindranath Tagore (*Rabindranath: Ek Asamanwito Dwandwo*, "Rabindranath: An Unresolved Tension", Sahitya Samavaya, Dhaka, Bangladesh; 2nd edn., Ebong Mushayera, Kolkata,

2015). Taking those texts as a point of departure (see below for some of the connections), the present monograph, drafted in 1988, articulated the conceptual basis of the practices that made the *Spandan* enterprise worthwhile.

One key philosophical insight informing those practices was the thought that exchanging feelings and thoughts with one's friends, in the light-hearted manner characteristic of informal conversations but with the seriousness that only such a context is able to underwrite, is a uniquely valuable mode of exploring questions because it alone nurtures the growth of personal accountability in its participants. As a philosopher who was later trained in psychology as well, Manashi took the stand that the capabilities of this mode, as a site for the development of personal responsibility and accountability in these domains, go well beyond what the institutional structures of the universities or the journals can possibly support, given the masks that formal academia forces on participants in its jousts. She articulates this stand in several writings in Bengali – most explicitly in her 1990 paper "Sakhya-priti, prem-kamana o anibarya Sigmund Freud (Friendship/affection, love/eros and the inevitable Sigmund Freud)", *Jiggasa* 11:3.287-301, where she argues that friendship is a metaproject, a crucible within which projects can be launched; and that it is this structural fact that makes it difficult to make friends if one is a very young child, not yet able to understand what projects are, or a very old adult, no longer willing to launch any. In the context of that argument, she takes on Freud's claim that all acts of friendship are nothing but sublimated manifestations of eros: she suggests that such a claim mixes up issues of origin with issues of use and that it ignores the metaproject character of friendship bonds. The present monograph can be read as a book-length unpacking of that argument and of the engagement with Freud.

To return to the connections between this monograph and

earlier writings, it is relevant to note that her monograph on Tagore argued that his project took the form of a convivial institution, but that his practices were unable to shed the hierarchical baggage he had inherited in several senses of this term. Her 1977 book on society and the mind, and her 2003 book on women (*Meyeder Bhumika o Bhashya*, "Rules and Roles for Women", Dasgupta, Kolkata; now republished, together with *Samaj-Mon*, as *Samaj-Mon o Nari-Bhashya*, Samatat, Kolkata, 2011) articulated a variety of specific theses around the project of conceptualizing an interpersonal order in which accountability requests would be formulated in a conversational tone and in a relaxed but earnest context ensuring sustainable compliance with such requirements.

In the global post-context in which we are reading the monograph today, perhaps we can best approach the text by underscoring the author's sense that reasonable adults not only work together, but also inquire together, an inquiry set in the interpersonal framework of their self-exploration, towards a reasonable aggregation of interpersonal adjustments that will be in everybody's interest – her sense that no theoretician working today has a magic wand either of rationality or of spiritual insight that can tell adults how best to balance the contradictory priorities that beset such inquiry. As things stand, our legacy from the "war of all against all" that had put the war machines known as states and their spokespersons in power is our addiction to macro-social doctrines. From those doctrines it follows that the micro-social is merely a site of a dishing out, decided on high, of goodies that the real masters alone truly own and understand. Thus, the only level at which micro-social actors can act fully rationally, with implications for the polis, is when they are aggregating with other micro-social groups of actors in the mode of a permanent constituent assembly, which alone has the right to create macro congregations. The struggle against these "macro"-based doctrines is not to be waged as a war. Our understanding of friendship places us in the tricky role of having to work against those doctrines gently, while continuing to be active and mutually trusting friends with their proponents, even if most of those proponents are convinced that we should all be engaged in a war of all against all and that friendships are merely strategies. How does one – not just interpersonally, but in philosophical dialogue with fellow thinkers who disagree – direct one's friendships peacewards, even under the shadow of the strategic view of friendship and cute gadgets and practices institutionalizing this cynicism? If we allow this question to trouble us, Manashi Dasgupta will have been understood.

Probal Dasgupta

Contents

Biographical Note

TO PRESENT Manashi Dasgupta's trajectory (b. Krishnanagar, 5 November 1928, d. Kolkata, 15 December 2010) involves pulling together the academic, cultural and critical strands of a vision that cherishes friendship and intercontextual conversation. It is at this crucial interface, she suggests, that the democratic imagination must make interpersonal sense of institutions. Her University of Calcutta master's degrees in philosophy (1951) and in psychology (1954) equipped her with an interdisciplinary background that led to her 1962 Cornell University doctoral dissertation *Some determinants of the judgement of "interestingness"*. In that contribution to social psychology she proposes that we imagine narratives about people we meet; perceiving a half-story leaves us intrigued and interested in the protagonist. Her interdisciplinary research sponsored by ICPR – a study of India's literary and institutional handling of love and friendship – is reported in the present monograph; here and in other texts, her interpersonalist vision identifies a democratic, anti-hierarchical imagination as a prerequisite for modernity; the point is to fashion a friendship-based institutional format outside the patriarchal family. In *Samaj-Mon* (Society and the Mind) and *Monostattwo o Rajniti* (Psychology and Politics), she stresses one India-specific question: how to build a family-independent civic episteme that will make nepotism look unnatural.

The academic flows into the cultural in Manashi's work. Her post-Cornell experiences in India convinced her that there was a disconnect between what the apparatus of psychology offers and what her fellow citizens would accept. She detected a widespread denial about the existence and addressability of basic interpersonal problems. Her response was a series of interventions – combining the artistic with the administrative in unusual ways – outside the institutional structures of psychology.

Her favourite art was vocal music. As one of Debabrata Biswas's early students, she became an exponent of Rabindrasangeet. But her knowledge of the diversity of Bengal's musical traditions made her want to represent that diversity rather than Tagore alone. Accordingly, Dasgupta focused on Tagore's contemporaries like Atul Prasad Sen (whose *ami tomar dhorbo na hat* and *mon re amar* she chose for her 1970 HMV single), Rajanikanta Sen, Dwijendra Lal Roy. Her knowledge of *kīrtana*s and of Bengali film music from the 1930s was encyclopaedic. Her academic and administrative career framed her artistic interventions. She taught philosophy at Deshabandhu College for Women, Kolkata (1956-57), served as Principal of Shri Shikshayatan College, Kolkata (1963-72, with a brief interlude as Regional Officer of the US Educational Foundation in India), where she initiated musical performance and discussion on an unusual scale. Her next job was to run and upgrade archiving and research at Rabindra Bhavana, Visva-Bharati, Santiniketan (1972-82, with a brief interlude as lecturer in psychology at the University of Calcutta). Here she enabled, and herself carried out, research on Tagore that took on board the intricate interpersonal context of his flourishing. Her book *Rabindranath: Ek Asamanwito Dwandwo* (Rabindranath: An Unresolved Tension) portrays a Tagore trying to bypass the vertical family and establish horizontal structures, but resorting to reverse nepotism as the means to this end, and bequeathing his crown of thorns to his son Rathindranath. This point, however, is embedded in an overall argument that analyses Tagore's textual and institutional oeuvre and concludes that he wished to build friendly institutions but had to work with colleagues steeped in patriarchal verticality. Significantly, Manashi had this study published in Dhaka (it has since been republished in Kolkata). She was one of the many cultural activists who played a role, especially from 1971 onwards, in promoting dialogue between the two Bengals – yet another inter-contextual conversation where she provided distinctive input.

We turn now to the third, critical strand in her contribution. Manashi's work combined criticism of patriarchy with a pervasive skepticism about simple-minded radical genres of opposition. She put herself at stake: the public in 1969 were hardly prepared to accept a woman testifying in court to defend Buddhadeva Bose's 1967 novel *Rat Bhore Brishti* (English translation by Clinton B. Seely, *Rain through the Night*, Hind Pocket Books, Delhi, 1973) against the charge of obscenity. What distinguished her work, including her 2003 book on "the roles and rules of women" (see the preface for bibliographic details), from familiar feminisms was her resolve to continue the work of figures she admired both in fiction and in social analysis, especially Ashapurna Debi (she wrote a biography of Ashapurna Debi for Sahitya Akademi) and Iravati Karve. Manashi's publications on the sociology of caste and on the way canonical literary texts deal with women are in self-conscious dialogue with Karve's work in these domains. And the sense in which her fiction constitutes a set of self-conscious sequels to Ashapurna Debi's work becomes clear from the fact that Binu, the protagonist in her first novel *Bhela* (Raft), is handicapped – she has a wooden leg.

Her other novels – *Trinoguccho* (Tufts of Grass), *Preme Apreme Nae* (Not in Love or Unlove), *Anarabdho* (The Sacrament that Failed), *Ghumonto Gharbari* (Sleeping Homes) – as well as her shorter fiction and autobiographical writings, explore themes that come to the fore once the screaming headlines have been digested. Manashi's worry, made explicit in several of these texts, is that populist voices will keep reiterating the headlines and pre-empt reflection at the level of theory, leading to broad-spectrum, unfocused social interventions and an excessive concentration on inequality at the expense of difference.

Author's Introduction

EVERY beginning has a beginning, in so far as human projects are concerned. Rabindranath in his inimitable style compares this process to that of "getting the wicks ready at dawn to have the lamps lighted at dusk".[1] The inquiry reported here also started out in that mode. Let me begin the narration by recalling the moments when my attention was first focused on two significant personalities of the nineteenth century: Sigmund Freud (1856–1939) and Rabindranath Tagore (1861–1941).

Tagore was a household word when I grew up in the 1930s in Calcutta; his name gradually gained even greater importance as years passed by. Freud was hardly known in this part of the world in the 1930s except in the departments of psychology and his name was, for all practical purposes, banned in respectable households. Youthful littérateurs and a handful of academicians knew of Freud. The situation has not substantially changed even today. I came to read him as a

---

1 Rabindranath Tagore, 1941, *Jogajog*, in his *Rabindra-Rachanavali*, Calcutta: Visva-Bharati, vol. 9.

[***Note from the editor, Probal Dasgupta***: While Manashi Dasgupta's print edition based references have been retained for the sake of authenticity, as has her style of referencing, most readers today will want to look the sources up on the web; for Tagore, the best online access at the moment of editing is through http://bichitra.jdvu.ac.in/index.php. Given this resource, several footnotes become redundant; I have retained them mainly in order to give the reader a sense of where the author found referencing necessary and where she did not.]

student, first of Mental and Moral Philosophy, and later of Psychology. During those years, we came to know of Gandhiji inquiring about the "Philosophy of Sigmund Freud" from the former's secretary, Nirmal Kumar Bose and felt somewhat puzzled that anyone of the stature of Nirmal Kumar Bose would not inform Gandhiji that Freud was no philosopher in a proper sense of the word. This was true of Tagore as well: the orthodox circle of academics would not accept him as a philosopher.

Tagore and Freud differed in their vocation and outlook; but they also had something in common to which I would like to draw my reader's attention. Freud's recognized role was that of a doctor, and Tagore's was that of a poet; however, they both crossed the boundaries of their roles to express their concern – each in his own way – about the predicament of the individual-in-society. Freud's *Civilisation and its Discontents*[2] can be read along with Tagore's *Crisis in Civilisation*[3] even today to advance our understanding of the nature of the wounds inflicted by civilization on hapless human beings locked into social frames.

Social frames differ from place to place and time to time. India and Western Europe in the nineteenth century came

---

[2] Sigmund Freud, 1930, *Civilisation and its Discontents* (tr. Joan Riviere), Standard Edition, vol. XXI, 1961.

[*Note from the editor*: See remarks appended to note 1.]

[3] Tagore's *Crisis in Civilisation: A Message on His Completing Eighty Years*, by Rabindranath Tagore (authorized translation, revised by the author), May 1941, pp. 1-11. The concluding section runs: "As I look around, I see the crumbling ruins of a proud civilisation strewn like a vast heap of futility. And yet I shall not commit the grievous sin of losing faith in Man. I would rather look forward to the opening of a new chapter in his history after the cataclysm is over and the atmosphere rendered clean with the spirit of service and sacrifice (. . .)." He ends his message with a quotation from the sacred book of Manu.

closer than ever before for reasons which will be duly discussed in the section on the contemporary social climate in India in Chapter 3. It is of interest to note that the Vienna experienced by Freud in the 1850s was not totally different from the Calcutta in which Tagore lived in the 1860s. Although Tagore did grow up in Calcutta, as a child he was prevented from getting the full taste of the life of the city by the walls of family pride and protectiveness. Much of the wealth had departed from their home by the time Tagore was born; his grandfather had died; his father was not as interested in adding to the family resources as he was in revitalizing the spiritual heritage of India by launching a religious movement to save the young from the lure of Christian missions. Tagore was initiated into reciting sacred texts by his father, who also protected the young Tagore from the drudgery and pain of going to a school where he was subjected to teasing and jokes. When Freud was growing up in Vienna, the city was throbbing with intellectual activities, which, however, were quite beyond his reach as he was a Jewish child, and a poor one too, due to his father's lack of success in business. Freud did not remember much of his childhood when he wrote about his early years in Vienna, perhaps because he did not wish to.[4] He recalled with distaste that in school his surname became a subject of incessant jokes, which caused him considerable distress (there were allusions, which recurred in his dreams, to *die Freude*, joy, and prostitutes).[5] When Tagore wrote his reminiscences, he did not seem to recall many of the factual details of his own childhood, either; but instead of setting his childhood aside as an unpleasant period, he took special care to add cheerful colour to all that he remembered that had aroused his poetic imagination. This was his way throughout his itinerary: to

4 Didier Anzieu, 1986, *Freud's Self-Analysis* (tr. Peter Graham), London: Hogarth Press and Institute of Psychoanalysis, p. 16.

5 Ibid.

speak of the good things of life, removing the depressing aspects from the account as much as possible, as if he was wishing them away. That style helped him to remain an "incurable optimist", which Freud was not.

Are there neutral criteria that would enable us to choose between these attitudes? Russell treats us to a witty comment:

> Optimism assumes, or attempts to prove, that the universe exists to please us and pessimism that it exists to displease us. Scientifically, there is no evidence that it is concerned with us one way or the other.[6]

No relevant facts, then, only attitudes: the optimist accepts the universe as it is, and feels happy about it, while the pessimist resists such acceptance. Tagore and Freud were perhaps equally convinced of the indifference of the universe to human affairs; but they remained differently disposed towards this indifference, which is what made them different. Tagore accepted the universe and its lack of concern with due humility and, in humility, he shared a common fate with others. Freud, on the other hand, focused his analytical scrutiny on the fact that human beings expect the universe to have concern for human life and well-being, even though human beings, in general, have very little mutual concern, very little willingness to help other persons; in this inquiry, he stood apart.

Tagore and Freud shared the same time span, spread over the world wars – Second World War was well into its second year by the time Tagore died. Freud did not live to see the devastation of that war at all, but as a Jew in Austria in the 1930s he had the scars imprinted on him even before the war truly broke out. After Freud's death in London, Auden wrote:

---

6 Bertrand Russell, 1948, *History of Western Philosophy and its Connection with Political and Social Circumstances from the Earliest Times to the Present Day*, London: George Allen and Unwin, 3rd impression, p. 787.

When there are so many we shall have to mourn,
when grief has been made so public, and exposed
to the critique of a whole epoch
the frailty of our conscience and anguish,
of whom shall we speak? For every day they die
among us, those who were doing us some good,
who knew it was never enough but
hoped to improve a little by living.

Such was this doctor. . .[7]

– And what did this doctor do? He

showed us what evil is, not, as we thought,
deeds that must be punished, but our lack of faith,
our dishonest mood of denial,
the concupiscence of the oppressor.[8]

A voice of reason is lost – that was the main refrain of the funeral lament of the grief-stricken world that had known Freud. Tagore's was a voice of a healer. With him the world lost a man who worked to bring about balance and beauty, to overcome discrepancies. The two voices never blended, though each in its own way left an indelible mark on our way of life bound by forces of love and friendship. The following pages are to bear witness to this.

In their lifetime Tagore and Freud met once, face to face, in Vienna – in October 1926, a crucial moment if we keep in view the crisis unfolding in Europe; and yet, nothing happened between them. Tagore had yet to fully grasp what Europe was going through, or what it meant to be a Jewish intellectual in Vienna in 1926. He was in his element, filling the gaps in his busy schedule of speaking assignments by writing letters and

---

[7] W.H. Auden, 1966, "In Memory of Sigmund Freud (d. September, 1939)", *Collected Shorter Poems 1927-1957*, London: Faber and Faber.

[8] Ibid.

composing songs. As for Freud, he was engaged in drafting his vigorous attack on religion that appeared in 1927: *The Future of an Illusion*. How would Tagore have reacted to Freud's views, had the latter chosen to open up that afternoon? It would be futile to speculate. Already in the grip of irreversible cancer in his mouth, Freud remained distant and was merely polite to Tagore, a Nobel laureate from British India on a lecture tour. Excessively good manners often block warmth. The two great minds were not able to break the ice, not even up to the point where the conversation would turn to topics of shared interest, such as Goethe, whose poetry each admired intensely without knowing that the other did so as well – let alone matters of social concern that were important to both of them. Had they permitted their inner anxieties to surface instead of just making polite conversation, perhaps Tagore's *Crisis in Civilisation* would have ended differently. There is, of course, no room whatsoever for any conjecture about Tagore's producing any change in Freud's *The Future of an Illusion*. Readers are well aware of his response to Romain Rolland's intervention[9] along the lines that one would expect Tagore to have taken if he were to react to *The Future of an Illusion*. Freud conceded no ground to speculative observations – no matter how colourful and deep – and insisted on subjecting every bit of (overt) spoken material to the rigour of analysis. Freud's uncompromising stand on scientific procedure will be discussed in Chapter 1, along with his view of "love". He was critical, one might say ruthless, about human sentiments which surfaced as noble and selfless. Perhaps Richard Wollheim is correct in his assumption that "Freud was never a lover of humanity"[10] which, we all know, Tagore always remained.

[9] Freud began his *Civilisation and its Discontents* with a reference to Romain Rolland's letter and a brief reply to it in which he politely rejected Rolland's argument based on "the primary nature of" what could be described as the "oceanic feeling".

[10] Richard Wollheim, 1971, *Freud*, London: Fontana, 6th impression, 1980.

Freud's lack of love for humanity did not stop him from appreciating the "richness and mystery of the psyche"[11] or observing that "mysticism is the obscure self-perception of the realm outside the ego, of the id".[12] He never refused to accept such private experiences as authentic;[13] but he did refuse to deal with such psychic moments at the level of analysis, for he took the stand that it did not make sense to attempt analysis under conditions of inadequate access. He did not "believe" in events and experiences inaccessible to psychoanalytic investigation. He avoided metaphysical overtones in his statements with particular care; this trait made him similar to modern poets who are romantically anti-romantic.[14] Suniti Kumar Chattopadhyay in his account quotes a modern *Magyar* (Chattopadhyay uses this endogenous term for "Hungarian") poet, Dezsö Kosztolányi, in English translation. His poem *Last Cry* reminded Chattopadhyay of Freud:

I believe in nothing,
If I die, I shall be nothing,
Even as before I was born
Upon this sunlit earth. Monstrous!
Soon I shall call you for the last time,
Be my good mother, O eternal darkness.[15]

---

[11] Richard Wollheim, op. cit., p. 218.

[12] Ibid., Freud quoted from Standard Edition XXIII.

[13] Professor Suniti Kumar Chatterji of ODBL fame (the Bengali form of his name is Suniti-Kumar Chattopadhyay) met Freud in Europe and reported his conversations bearing on this point. See his *Paschimer Yatri* (a travelogue in Bengali), Calcutta: Mitra and Ghosh, 1372 BE [Bengali Era; 1372 BE = CE 1965-66], pp. 45-54.

[14] For an elaboration of the idea of romantic anti-romanticism, see Abu Sayeed Ayyub, 1968, *Adhunikata o Rabindranath*, 2nd edn., Calcutta: Dey's, 1971, pp. 24-25, 35.

[15] Chattopadhyay, op. cit.

There is, however, a basic difference missed by Chattopadhyay, one that helps key us into the spirit of Freud's work. Freud would never have imagined the "nothing" as "monstrous". He refrained from expressing emotions about what he recognized as scientific fact; otherwise he would never have been able to go in for self-analysis. Even hostile readers are bound to notice that Freud's theories remained more or less open-ended and incomplete in many respects as he was less interested in systematization and kept waiting to have more facts, carefully screened through *analysis*, to "complete" his picture. Tagore looked for, and found, complete pictures in what he saw. His was a vision of *synthesis*.

That the scientist Freud and the poet Tagore, both city-bred (though protected in a certain sense from the impact of the city) and products of nineteenth-century romanticism, should differ widely in the way they spelled "love" is not surprising. What does surprise me is that both of them have continued to exert direct or indirect influence on generations of Indians throughout the twentieth century in the context of dealing with love and friendship as concepts or as experiences, without this influence being openly recognized. Freud's presence, when recognized, is resented. This is due not only to the fact that Freud's libido is distressingly self-seeking but also to his identification of the destructive death-instinct in the human psyche[16] as a basic, pervasive component. If talking about sex is loathsome, death is a frightening topic for ordinary people, rich or poor; that these are natural phenomena does not mean that one is free to bring them up; if they are to be mentioned, one needs carefully coded linguistic cover to avoid sounding offensive or indecent. Freud offered none: uncovering hidden levels of stress was his mission. Tagore's cover was poetic-spiritual – to which I turn in Chapter 4. In

[16] Sigmund Freud, 1920, *Beyond the Pleasure Principle*. His "death instinct" hypothesis is proposed in this book.

the same chapter, I introduce (Sri) Aurobindo, another significant personality of nineteenth-century Bengal who was born in Calcutta in 1872, was educated in England and lived for most of his life in Pondicherry, where he died. His eminence as a mystical sage overshadowed the rest of his personality for most observers. But Aurobindo blended three different personalities: that of a romantic poet, of a political revolutionary and of a mystical philosopher. That his serious and significant views about love and death have not been given due importance in serious discussion in India, outside the hagiographic circles of Auroville and the Aurobindo Ashram, is partly because his writings were addressed primarily to the elite who knew English and had at least some familiarity with the scientific theories and discoveries of the West. Another reason was suggested to me by Professor Sisir Kumar Ghosh when we met; I entirely agree with him on this point. Written in a poetic form, (Sri) Aurobindo's views need elucidation and explication. Barring a few exceptions (e.g. Prof. Ghosh himself), persons familiar with (Sri) Aurobindo's theories have not made an effort to communicate his message to the public.

Juxtaposing (Sri) Aurobindo with Tagore, rather than with religious leaders like Ramakrishna or Saibaba, is one way of affirming his place among the independent social thinkers of modern India. Although it is clothed in a mystical-metaphysical cover, Aurobindo's idea of love is no repetition of the traditional view. Speaking of "love" as "man's lien on the Absolute"[17] Aurobindo saturates love with a degree of

---

[17] Sri Aurobindo, 1970, *Savitri: A Legend and a Symbol*, Pondicherry: Sri Aurobindo Ashram, 4th Complete edn.

[***Note from the editor***: This passage is available in the 1997 edition of *The Complete Works*, vols. 33-34, p. 633; since Manashi Dasgupta's references to (Sri) Aurobindo's writings highlight specific passages, and since readers are bound to look them up on the web, I have supplied 1997 edition page numbers for all references to his writings.]

metaphysicality that would perhaps strike both Freud and Tagore as unacceptable. He appears to do this in order to resist Freudian attempts to place the forces of love on a par with those of death. Although Aurobindo hardly ever mentions Freud in any of his writings, the way the figure of Death in his portrayal asserts that "Man has no other help but only Death" reminds the reader of Freud's observations. In the face of this annihilating force, Aurobindo's *Savitri* stands firm and powerful; she says:

> *My love is not a craving of the flesh,*
> *It came to me from God, to God returns.*[18]

(Sri) Aurobindo is a systematic philosopher. In his books and statements he presents a whole scheme of ideas in consistency with his basic faith in the divine principle and the principle of evolution. Tagore too spoke of evolution, but in a very different style; and Freud's approach to evolution was of course entirely different.

At the personal level, Rabindranath Tagore and Aurobindo Ghosh knew each other and had significant friends in common (e.g. Sister Nivedita). Their approaches to the critical problems facing the country and its people were different, however, and became increasingly so with the passage of time. Tagore's poem[19] inspired by his deep appreciation for Aurobindo's rebellious patriotism is an authentic document of the poet's respect for this leader of the people. He was reportedly eager to have a meeting of minds with Aurobindo in Pondicherry and to exchange views on how isolation might prove helpful for those of them engaged in the quest for a deeper self-understanding – a project that

---

[18] Sri Aurobindo [passage available in the 1997 edition, vols. 33-34, p. 612 – Editor's note].

[19] *Namaskar* (a poem by Rabindranath Tagore) was written in Santiniketan, in August 1907.

they had both had been pursuing, away from the city, in Santiniketan and Pondicherry.[20] The distance between them, however, proved impossible to bridge; the two ashrams remained very different in terms of institutional style as well as aims and objectives. Mrs. (Mirra) Richard, who was later to become the Mother at Aurobindo Ashram, Pondicherry, was reportedly asked by Tagore when they met in Japan in the year 1919 to come and "take charge of" Santiniketan. She declined the offer.[21] Even if she had accepted, even if we imagine a state of affairs in which she was present in Santiniketan, Tagore's ashram, in all probability, would have remained distant, in terms of its goals and its methods of pursuing them, from the ashram in Pondicherry. The difference between the two lay in the idea of community and the concept of power that the founders of these institutions cherished.

Love and friendship develop within the fold of communities, administered and ruled over by authority (power). This alone does not provide any clue to my readers as to why I should emphasize the nineteenth-century social perspective at the outset of my inquiry. Love and friendship are hardly modern products of the nineteenth century! In India we have numerous legends, folklore texts, classical drama and early lyrical poetry eloquently affirming love. Indian epics and tales portrayed friendship in rich colours long before the Western "romantic revolt" came to prominence in the spheres of literature, politics and philosophy and converged into its nineteenth-century form familiar to us. Yet there is no denying that love and friendship, as well as the communities within

---

[20] Professor Amiya Kumar Chakravarty (1901-86), an eminent modern Bengali poet, who had served as secretary to Tagore for some years, narrated this episode to me in a personal interview at Santiniketan, 1978.

[21] Navajata, 1972, *Sri Aurobindo*, National Biography Series, Delhi: National Book Trust, 1972, p. 64.

which they develop, undergo changes not only in form but also in what Freud would describe as "manifest content". Literary creations, fantasies, conceptual formulations and personal responses record gradual changes. The more dramatic changes, often marking the end of an epoch, are to be seen through conflicting thoughts and ideas, emerging ideologies and mental and behavioural confusion at the level of ordinary people. In nineteenth-century Calcutta, such disruption, tension and excitement were in the air.[22]

Traditional India with its unperturbed continuity may not have been at its best in 1757 when foreign military power, in the form of the East India Company, won a decisive battle in Plassey, Bengal. However, what we find in the sophistication of Bharatchandra[23] or in the unadorned simplicity of Ramprasad Sen[24] in the eighteenth century can still be viewed as a continuation of the old culture seeking expression through subtly changed rhetoric and idiom. In contrast, the nineteenth century witnessed a real take-off, with a new ideology of universal humanism embodied in the life and activities of Raja Rammohun Roy (1772–1833). Rammohun was not a product

[22] Sibnath Sastri, 1955, *Ramtanu Lahiri o Tatkalin Banga Samaj*, Calcutta: New Age, 2nd edn. 1957; Dilip Kumar Biswas, 1983, *Rammohan Samiksha*, Calcutta: Saraswat Prakashan.

[23] Bharat Chandra Roy Gunakar (1712-60), widely honoured and known for his epic *Annadamangal*, was a court poet at Krishnanagar during the rule of Krishna Chandra Roy. He hailed from Howrah.

[24] Ramprasad Sen (1720-82), a contemporary of Nawab Sirazuddaula (1733-57), remembered for his devotional songs composed in praise of Kālī. His unique melody, set to *ektāl* and known as the "Rāmprasādī", has been used since his time by several major songwriters of Bengal, including Tagore. Ramprasad Sen was born in Halishahar; he used to visit Calcutta, where he had admiring patrons such as Chudamoni Datta. Ramprasad lived through the Battle of Plassey as well as the devastating famine of 1176 BE (CE 1770) in Bengal under the rule of the East India Company.

but a producer of the nineteenth-century Indian social climate. He never systematized his ideas of universal humanism – the way it all turned out, this became Tagore's task. But Rammohun's ideas of religious and social reform, his friendships with Indians and non-Indians young and old, and finally his founding of the Brahma-Sabha (the Brahmo-Samaj) in 1828 – making it accessible for worship and prayer to everyone irrespective of denominational and/or caste identities (barring only idol-worshippers) – posed a serious challenge to traditional Indian society, which was trying to develop strategies for cultural self-defence against foreign settlers.

Rammohun challenged the traditionalists in the name of all that was best and noble in the tradition itself. This challenge of his, along with the introduction of English education, which exposed young students in India to the literature of revolt from the West, drastically terminated the earlier enterprise of gradual modification of Indian culture to adapt it to new situations. In the nineteenth century, Indians learnt how to make effective use of the technique and the vocabulary of the West both in the context of confronting Western rule in India and at the level of facing the world beyond the boundaries of their country. This was the time when, in response to the British "image of India", young Indians were earnestly in search of a true identity. Such a process had to be "in part reactionary, in part revolutionary", a romantic transvaluation of all that had been held in social esteem. Love and friendship too, as values and as practices, passed through a phase of turmoil, transforming Indian literary representations of love, of friendship and of the power (often taking the form of Death) ruling over friendship and love. That moment inaugurated a process that has not yet ended. Any valid study of love and friendship in Indian context has to begin at that moment, and to consider the outstanding literature of this period. This is not to suggest that pre-nineteenth-century materials are to be disregarded. I have tried to address both in my presentation of love and friendship in the Indian context.

My inquiry, while grappling with contemporary social conditions and norms, revolves around a specific question: how much of the ideal of the pre-modern past lingers in India today? In this quest, I have been greatly helped by men and women young and old participating in open-ended discussions, or exclusive interviews, or both. The observational data collected in this mode are reported in detail in Chapter 3. Whether my attempt to combine empirical findings with speculative discourse is of any value as a method of expanding our philosophical understanding of social processes is for the reader to decide. My modest aim, in this account that draws on some resources of narrative and analysis, is to bring some pertinent information to bear on our understanding of contemporary India.

1

Freud

Some Observations on the Man and His Theories

SPEAKING of desire and that which structures desire, Jacques Lacan makes an almost poetic utterance:

> that which is thus given to the Other to fill, and which is strictly that which it does not have, since it, too, lacks being, is what is called love, but it is also hate and ignorance.[1]

Freud would have been less poetic. He avoided complicated formulations wherever possible in his expositions; as a result his interpretative accounts of dreams, jokes, etc. often read like narratives with endless episodes and sub-plots. This is one reason for the prevailing misunderstanding of his Psychoanalysis, a misunderstanding aggravated by its frequent vulgarization by many authors who are convinced that a brief exposition can seriously introduce lay readers to what the field is all about. It is not clear, however, whether Lacan's style of interpretation offers a viable alternative to Freud's own approach (it would be disingenuous to pretend that Lacan is not proposing an alternative). "Lacan's Freudian revolution" has aroused a great deal of interest and touched off heated discussions among theorists of several disciplines. But within this circle of scholars, a certain degree of uneasiness is evident. Elizabeth Wright, for example, in her penetrating

[1] Jacques Lacan, 1977, *Ecrits: A Selection* (tr. Alan Sheridan), New York: W.W. Norton, p. 263.

analysis from the point of view of literary criticism, observes that:

> Lacan's own style, frustrating for the reader, continually mimes this illusion by means of puns, innuendos and outrageous conceits.[2]

The "illusion" she refers to will be taken up for discussion presently.

Jacques Lacan (1901-81), himself a psychoanalyst directing the *école freudienne* in Paris between 1964 and 1980, became accessible to the English-reading public only recently. The existentialist philosopher Jean-Paul Sartre (1905-80) – who was asked by an American film director to write a screenplay on Freud in 1958 – became widely known all over the world, including our own country, much earlier. Yet I begin my observations on Freud with this quotation from Lacan because, despite the difficulties of his style noted above, Lacan's reading of Freud nonetheless brings us closer to the heart of the matter than what Sartre presents as his own enterprise of "Ontological Psychoanalysis". The relevance of Anzieu's work – to which I turn in detail towards the end of this chapter – becomes clear only in the perspective of Lacan's "refining and reformulating the work of Sigmund Freud".[3] This is not to suggest that Sartre and his existential tenets do not deserve special mention in a meaningful discussion on Freud. The difference between existential analysis and Freudian psychoanalysis is of course well known, especially through Freud's correspondence with Ludwig Binswanger. Sartre was not actively engaged in existential analysis in the way Binswanger was. On the other

---

[2] Elizabeth Wright, 1984, *Psychoanalytic Criticism: Theory in Practice*, London: Methuen, p. 112.

[3] Juliet Mitchell, 1982, in her Introduction ("Feminine Sexuality") to *Feminine Sexuality: Jacques Lacan and the Ecole Freudienne*, ed. Juliet Mitchell and Jacqueline Rose, London: MacMillan, p. 1.

hand, it is worth noting that Sartre, in his critical comments about Freud,[4] took a very different line from his fellow existentialist Karl Jaspers.

Jaspers, responsible for bracketing Kierkegaard and Nietzsche for the first time, and also for announcing "the principal themes of existentialism" in 1919,[5] was essentially a medical man, like Freud. In his *Man in the Modern Age* (1931), he defined existentialism as "a philosophy which does not cognise objects" but "elucidates and makes actual the being of the thinker". He took a strong, uncompromising stand against philosophy and science having anything to do with each other. His rejection of Freud was based on this position he had taken. He found Freud (as well as Marx) guilty of putting forward world-views in the guise of scientific theories. It may be of interest to note that Jaspers found even Charles Darwin's work unacceptable, suggesting that:

> man has always existed, although perhaps in a different biological form, and that the ape is a degenerate man. For all Jaspers' respect for science, he completely rejects scientific conclusions not only when they are philosophy in disguise, which is his official ground for objecting, but whenever they threaten the conception of a man-centred universe.[6]

Jaspers' allegation that Freud was upholding "a barren hateful world-view concealed behind a humanitarian form" has no basis in fact, for Freud never made any specifically humanitarian proposals, and more generally he had no world-view at all: he decried the general demand for a comprehensive positive world-view in scientific inquiry. In his view, a scientist could not possibly settle down cosily with

---

4 Jean-Paul Sartre, 1985, *The Freud Scenario* (tr. Quintin Hoare), ed. J.B. Pontalis, London: Verso.

5 John Passmore, 1968, *A Hundred Years of Philosophy* [Duckworth, 1957], Harmondsworth: Penguin, repr. 1970, chapter 19.

6 Ibid., pp. 471-72.

a *weltanschauung*. He observed:

> Only believers, who demand that science shall be a substitute for the catechism they have given up, will blame an investigator for developing or even transforming his views.[7]

Sartre had no reservation about "developing or even transforming" one's views as long as one remained *authentic*, focused at all times on one's capacity for free *choice*. Anyone who reacted to the world of events as if things were happening to him was suffering from bad faith. In Sartre's scheme of things, nothing could possibly be a truly compelling force in the empirical world unless the individual involved perceived it as compelling, and such perceiving represented a choice. It is not surprising, then, that Sartre would see Freud as "a doctrinaire and somewhat limited *chef d'école*, a mediocre philosopher none of whose concepts would stand up to scrutiny (. . .)."[8] The idea which Sartre espoused – that there are no innocent victims, so to speak, that whatever happens to the individual stems from his existential choice – hardly has anything cheerful about it. Yet, instead of being criticized and rejected as a pessimist, Sartre was acclaimed as a profound thinker because there was a certain heroism in his statement of the existentialist viewpoint. The appeal of Sartre to a large extent lay in his ability to arouse a sense of self-respect and human dignity among men. His view that those who fail to see that man is what he makes of himself are caught in self-deception is challenging; adults capable of intellection seem to feel addressed by this challenge. Freud's project of discovering the process of man's making of himself takes an entirely different route. His method, being empirical, did not permit him to disregard any data made available to him through direct observation. He did, of course, talk of observed

7 Freud, 1920, "Beyond the Pleasure Principle", Standard Edition, vol. XVIII, p. 6.

8 Sartre, op. cit., Pontalis, in Editor's preface, p. xii.

materials in conceptual terms, because discourse necessarily involves concepts. But he did not begin with preconceived notions about man's capacity to transcend his limits. His dispassionate observations, exposing as they did the presence of basic infantile urges in adults who carefully (or sometimes not so carefully) covered them up, posed a threat to adults whose grown-up self-image was precariously built on their ability to suppress those very urges.

Sartre's account of human anxiety arising out of what he portrayed as the impossible task facing man, that is, to choose on everybody's behalf and through this choice to *be* himself, was strangely inspiring. What he (and other existentialists) sought was *the individual* who must achieve his authentic identity through his free choice, undetermined by any prescription by others and undefined by pre-existing essential characteristics. This quest is comparable to the nineteenth-century romantics' yearning for free individuality; the feeling of existential isolation (and despair) is also reminiscent of the romantic preoccupation with agony and loneliness. Kaplan makes the point that for existentialism "loneliness is a metaphysical category. (. . .) it is derived from the existential analysis of the human condition, not of contemporary society."[9] Alienation thus forms an inalienable aspect of the human condition; it is to escape from this predicament that man seeks allies, but the theory of existentialism provides little room for human alliance. The authentic individual cannot reach others without risking the loss of freedom and integrity, because proximity undermines individuality – unless, of course, the individual is ready to deceive others in order to please them. Neither Sartre nor any other existentialist of repute appeared to be troubled over this theoretical problem. Finally, Kaplan's observation, formulated in a tone of respectful sympathy, sounds compelling:

---

[9] Abraham Kaplan, 1961, *The New World of Philosophy*, New York: Vintage, p. 112.

> (. . .) the existentialist (. . .) is really a kind of amateur literary psychologist. (. . .) This is what gives his philosophy such a human content, such relevance to the things that trouble people just because they are people, not cosmologists or logicians. (. . .) existentialism does not pursue psychology as a branch of science for which human behavior is a part of nature to be analyzed and explained as other natural phenomena are. Its psychology has more kinship with literature and the stage than with scholarship and the laboratory.[10]

It was a significant coincidence that Sartre came closer to Freud through his commitment to writing drafts of the screenplay in 1959-60. Pontalis reports:

> While he was reading Jones's book, I recall having heard him say with real delight, 'That Freud of yours, I must say, he was neurotic through and through'. At once, he was able to understand, if not accept, notions which previously, as a philosopher who had remained more Cartesian than he thought, he had pulled to pieces – notions such as those of unconscious thought or repression, (. . .) it seems to me undeniable that Sartre succeeded in making perceptible – hence first and foremost in making perceptible to himself – a certain number of phenomena which could no longer be adequately accounted for by the notion of 'bad faith' that he had long promoted to counter Freud.[11]

It is unlikely that Sartre was about to repudiate his existentialist position because of his better "understanding" of Freud: existentialism is more a way of life than a set of philosophical doctrines. Here we find a certain resemblance between existentialism and Buddhism – the latter being primarily a way of life though very differently conceived. The Buddhists' surrender to the "Sangha" has something distinctive about it. It is possible to argue that the spirit of surrender (to Dharma,

---

[10] Kaplan, op. cit., p. 113.

[11] Pontalis, op. cit.

Sangha and Buddha) is a later addition by followers of Buddha and has little or no connection with the basic tenets of Buddhism, but such an argument would have no direct bearing on our thesis. It is more useful for us to focus on another distinctive feature of Buddhism, viz. the conception of Desire (*taṇhā* in Pali, *tṛṣṇā* in Sanskrit). Buddha viewed *tanha*[12] (desire) as the core of human bondage that inevitably leads to suffering. This is identical to what Freud discovered: the fact that desire (*Wunsch*/wish) is situated at the root of neurotic ailments, which led Freud to his other discovery – the unconscious. The affinities between Freud's "wish" and Buddha's *trishna* are remarkable. What enabled Freud to move this inquiry into science was the crucial step of linking desire to the unconscious.

This is not to suggest that Freud was the first theorist to use the word "unconscious". Freud's contribution was to establish "the science of the mental unconscious", that is, "psychoanalysis". In his scientific quest he was admittedly indebted to predecessors and contemporaries in science proper. But his interest in archaeology and literature also nourished his scientific imagination. Drawing on this imagination enabled him to write analytical expositions whose "chief aim [was] to make no sacrifice to an appearance of being simple, complete or rounded off, or to disguise problems and not to deny the existence of gaps and uncertainties".[13] He was aware of and reconciled to the special challenge that psychologists would always have to face:

---

12 ***Editor's note:*** I am a professional linguist; I have given some thought to the transcription practices to be followed in such a text, and have steered a middle path between the Indologically accurate *taṇhā*/*tṛṣṇā* and the easily recognizable *tanha*/*trishna*; every transcribed or Romanized form represents a conscious choice on my part; criticism will still occur and is welcome.]

13 Freud, 1933/1932, Preface to *New Introductory Lectures on Psychoanalysis*, Standard Edition, vol. XXII.

> No reader of an account of astronomy will feel disappointed and contemptuous of the science if he is shown the frontiers at which our knowledge of the universe melts into haziness. Only in psychology is it otherwise. There mankind's constitutional unfitness for scientific research comes fully into the open. What people seem to demand of psychology is not progress in knowledge, but satisfaction of some other sort; every unsolved problem, every admitted uncertainty is made into a reproach against it. Whoever cares for the science of mental life must accept these injustices along with it.[14]

And what is more, the resonance of the critical comments by existentialists can often be heard in the assessments of psychoanalysis by others as well. His response to these assessments led to a style of writing that a perceptive author such as Juliet Mitchell characterizes as follows:

> though he claimed to be congenitally incapable of philosophic thought, we can see that the terms of his defence of his status of science for psychoanalysis and the words he chose for many of his concepts he developed within it are part of an ongoing contemporary argument about the philosophy of science during that period.[15]

None of this diminishes the value or significance of Freud's contribution to science. Most commentators would agree with Lee and Herbert's willingness to rank Freud with Copernicus or Darwin. They revolutionized our idea of man. Man used to enjoy a privileged position on our "special" planet earth until the discoveries of these three came to be widely acknowledged. Scientific revolutions do not bring peace; knowledge is disturbing to ordinary people. Only those who in their search for knowledge find inquiry itself rewarding are able to remain enthusiastic about the progress of science contributing "to the dethronement of Man's confidence in

---

[14] Freud, 1933/1932, op. cit.

[15] Juliet Mitchell, 1974, *Psychoanalysis and Feminism*, Harmondsworth: Penguin, repr. 1976, Introduction, p. xx.

himself as being of unique importance in the universe".[16] Freud's effort to shed light on deeper terrains of the human psyche had this destabilizing impact, even though in this enterprise he played the role of a special kind of leader to a subcommunity of scientists. The subcommunity that accepted his leadership was not just a community of analysts, but of analysands as well. Analysis was not an external intervention. Freud was his own patient (analysand) from 1895 onwards. This self-analysis, performed with a view to ascertaining the validity of other empirical findings, could serve as a model for dispassionate research in mental science. Reacting to the question of allowing laymen (non-doctors) into the work of psychoanalysis, he asserted his position in favour of admitting laymen with special training in analysis on the grounds that psychoanalysis should not be "swallowed up by medicine"; his major interest was *knowing*, not curing. He was indeed looking forward to the prospect that some day psychoanalysis,

> [a]s a theory of 'depth-psychology', a theory of the mental unconscious, (. . .) can become indispensable to all sciences which are concerned with the evolution of human civilisation and its major institutions such as art, religion and the social order.[17]

He was confident that a "cure" – which was, of course, his objective as a medical man – would only be brought about through knowledge and a better understanding of the ailment. He writes with candour:

> I became a doctor through being compelled to deviate from my original purpose; and the triumph of my life lies in my

[16] S.G.M. Lee and Martin Herbert (eds.), 1970, *Freud and Psychology: Selected Readings*, Harmondsworth: Penguin. Of the nineteen articles included in this book, fifteen are reports on experimentation with Freudian notions of psychic agencies, developmental stages and defence mechanisms.

[17] Freud, 1926, "The Question of Lay Analysis".

> having, after a long and roundabout journey, found my way back to my earliest path. I have no knowledge of having had any craving in my early childhood to help suffering humanity. My innate sadistic disposition was not a very strong one, so that I had no need to develop this one of its derivatives. Nor did I ever play the 'doctor-game'; my infantile curiosity evidently chose other paths. In my youth I felt an overpowering need to understand something of the riddles of the world in which we live and perhaps even to contribute something to their solution. The most hopeful means of achieving this end seemed to be to enroll myself in the medical faculty; but even after that I experimented – unsuccessfully – with Zoology and Chemistry, till at last, under the influence of Brucke, who carried more weight with me than anyone else in my whole life, I settled down to physiology, though in those days it was too narrowly restricted to histology. By that time I had already passed all my medical examinations, but I took no interest in anything to do with medicine till the teacher whom I so deeply respected warned me that in view of my impoverished material circumstances I could not possibly take up a theoretical career. Thus I passed from the histology of the nervous system to neuropathology and then, prompted by fresh influences, I began to be concerned with the neuroses. I scarcely think, however, that my lack of a genuine medical temperament has done much damage to my patients. For it is not greatly to the advantage of patients if their doctor's therapeutic interest has too marked an emotional emphasis. They are best helped if he carries out his task coolly and keeping as closely as possible to the rules.[18]

Freud was keenly conscious of an "inseparable bond" which existed in psychoanalysis between cure and research:

> It was impossible to treat a patient without learning something new.[19]

---

[18] Freud, 1927, Postscript to "The Question of Lay Analysis".

[19] Ibid.

What Freud meant to suggest was that the treatment helped both the analyst (the doctor, researcher) and the analysand (the patient, trainee) to learn something new (hidden and unrecognized so far) about psychic life, failing which the treatment would remain incomplete. In other words, the cure consists in the acquisition of knowledge of self in a proper perspective whereby one succeeds in identifying (recognizing) one's own private self, individualized in a very narrow, limited way yet universally present in every human being born to parents situated in culture.

Here we come to recognize the dichotomy between nature and culture into which every child is born. If love is seen as part of *life* in the sense of *participation in nature,* then it follows that we must also take this view in the case of hate, subsuming under it both "resentment" and the behavioural notion of "anger" recognized even by behaviourists. However, Freud does not encourage our inclination to equate the natural with the biological; biology as he understands it has nothing to do with either love nor hate; love and hate belong to psychic nature. In the unconscious, love and hate coexist. It is only culture that forbids this coexistence, thereby making demands concerning "love" for which nature per se cannot make any direct resources available. Lacan quotes from St. Augustine who "foreshadowed psychoanalysis" in expressing recognition of "the central nucleus of ambivalent aggressivity". The relevant passage (quoted here from Lacan's text) does indeed suggest that St. Augustine was given to dispassionate observation and was not bound by the stereotypes of his time:

> I have seen with my own eyes and known very well an infant in the grip of jealousy: he could not yet speak and already he observed his foster brother, pale and with an envenomed stare.[20]

[20] Lacan, op. cit.

Indian references similar to the one quoted above will be discussed in the next chapter. In the meantime, let us note that Freud had to reckon with the presence of "ambivalent aggressivity" in the unconscious in the pre-oedipal narcissistic phase. A critic such as Ian D. Suttie ignores the theory-internal character of these observations when he claims that "the Freudian [approach] is based on hate – a denial of love".[21] Suttie thinks he sees an inner inconsistency here, as in his opinion (as a practising psychoanalyst) the "healing of the mind" depends on the analyst's capacity to forge a bond of love (i.e. positive transference) with the patient. This is an interesting response to Freud's work. When Freud studied the phenomenon of transference[22] what struck him much more forcefully was actually the "negative therapeutic reaction", the resistance whose content Lacan formulates in these terms:

> I can't bear the thought of being freed by anyone other than myself.[23]

What kind of "freedom" is at stake in this thought? As a point of departure, no doubt, freedom from the pain of the ailment;

---

[21] Ian D. Suttie, 1935, *The Origin of Love and Hate*, London: Kegan Paul, 4th impression, 1948.

[22] "Transference" as a phenomenon is mentioned in the Freudian literature quite early, in the Breuer period, when Freud was yet to use the method of free association. Through transference of attachment (affect), a lost "object" can be replaced by another. In the analytical situation, the therapist takes the place of the "object" of desire (love) when the patient transfers his/her positive affect on to the therapist. The situation, however, may be reversed if the patient transfers his/her negative affect (hate/aggression). There is nothing pathological about transference as such. In ordinary life one often sees a bereaved mother developing a strong attachment with another child of her own child's age. She "transfers" her love and affection to this new "object" to fill the void created by the loss of her child to whom she was attached.

[23] Lacan, op. cit., p. 13.

but at a deeper level, freedom from certain misconstruals by the subject in its representation of self and related objects. This process of construing everything amiss (missing the point in terms of the perspective which reality-testing identifies as the only valid perspective) takes place in the unconscious. Resistance becomes operative when the release or satisfaction of an instinctual impulse in the conscious phase is blocked by what Freud would later call the "unconscious conscious". In his 1915 text on the unconscious, however, he presents a topographical point of view which demarcates the unconscious, preconscious and conscious as spatially separated systems of psychic life. Freud was aware that although

> Research has given irrefutable proof that mental activity is bound up with the function of the brain as it is with no other organ (. . .) every attempt to go on from there to discover a localisation of mental processes, every endeavour to think of ideas as stored up in nerve-cells and of excitations as travelling along nerve-fibres, has miscarried completely. The same fate would await any theory which attempted to recognise, let us say, the anatomical position of the system Cs. – conscious mental activity – as being in the cortex, and to localise the unconscious processes in the subcortical parts in the brain.

Having observed that research in anatomy was insufficiently advanced and that there was little that a psychologist could do to remedy this deficit, Freud concluded that psychical topography in psychoanalysis can have "*for the present* nothing to do with anatomy; it has reference not to anatomical localities but to regions in the mental apparatus, wherever they may be situated in the body".[24]

Fresh evidence from psychoanalytical investigation led Freud to reformulate his views in terms of the *id*, the *ego* and the *superego*, with the unconscious seen as structuring the total

[24] Freud, 1915, "The Unconscious", Standard Edition, vol. XIV.

personality. In 1915, the unconscious was kept separate from the conscious, each vying with the other system for primacy over affectivity "even within the limits of normal life". However, Mitchell's comments are applicable to this account as well:

> The unconscious that Freud discovered is not a deep, mysterious place, whose presence, in mystical fashion, accounts for all the unknown; *it is knowable and it is normal.* What it contains is normal thought, utterly transformed by its own laws (which Freud called the primary process), but nevertheless only transformed and hence still recognisable if one can deduce the manner of the transformation, that is, decipher the laws of the primary process to which thought is subjected. For instance, an unconscious wish originating in infancy becomes attached to the wish in the present time which has evoked it, but if it is unacceptable to consciousness, it is pushed down (repressed) into the unconscious where it is transformed and where it remains – until re-evoked, or until it breaks out (as a symptom) or until it is analysed (. . .) they are always there, speaking to us, in their way.[25]

The way unconscious ideas "speak to us", the way they are transformed, reflects the laws of the unconscious order: "exemption from mutual contradiction, primary process (mobility of cathexes), timelessness and replacement of external by psychical reality". The world of the unconscious is not mysterious, but it does defy adult rational principles: everything becomes possible; any object can stand for any other object (e.g. a thumb for a nipple); dreams count as true. "Defy" is however a premature word to use in this context. The unconscious is initially *unaware* of adult rules. Only when these are thrust upon the child through the perceptual system accessible only to consciousness, compelling the latter to adapt itself to the demands of reality by repressing instinctual urges,

[25] Mitchell, op. cit., pp. 6-7.

do the compulsions of rationality begin to matter. As the repressed material forms a layer of the unconscious which *can* become conscious (as these ideas have been recorded in the consciousness), the gap between the unconscious and the conscious begins to take shape in a psychic region that had been seamless; it is at that point that the question of surrender or defiance arises for the first time. Freud's discovery, the "Oedipus Complex", has to do with that moment in the child's development.

In order to see how Freud relates his view of unconscious ideas to his theory of libido, it is important to take a closer look at the pre-oedipal, pre-linguistic unconscious. How, on this approach, does the unconscious deal with unacceptable instinctual urges or impulses (unacceptable in the sense that discharge or release is prevented) during the period of infancy when there is "no cleavage between conscious and unconscious mental activity"? Freud suggests that at that stage "the task of fending off instinctual impulses is dealt with by the other vicissitudes which instincts may undergo – e.g. reversal into the opposite or turning round upon the subject's own self".[26] These mechanisms continue to remain operative even after "repression" has become active; they must, because repression cannot resolve or eliminate all conflicts of the psychic region.

The "reversal" mentioned above is of significance. So is Freud's distinction between repressible and irrepressible instinctual impulses. The instinctual impulses aiming at the satisfaction of hunger/thirst, and relieving the waste-products by urinating/defecating are so inalterably tied with the attainment of their objects that no diversion is possible. There is no scope for repression of these impulses. The question of modification of these impulses through habit-formation and

---

[26] Freud, 1915, "Instincts and Their Vicissitudes", Standard Edition, vol. XIV.

developmental techniques of conscious *suppression* must not be confused with *repression*. Repression takes place at the subjective level of the organism trying to settle the issues arising within the field of contact, visibility and sound patterns. At the subjective level of the unconscious where the inner and the outer are not differentiated, every bit of the field belongs (through representation, by way of ideas) to the subject: a body, a mass of "desire". With the emergence of conscious subjectivity, repression operates only on "desire", which is another name for the body (sexuality).

Freud envisaged two phases of repression. The primal phase came into action with "the psychical (ideational) representative of the instinct being denied entrance into the conscious". The second phase of *repression proper* which

> affects mental derivatives of the repressed representatives, or such trains of thought as, originating elsewhere, have come into associative connection with it. *On account of this association*, these ideas experience the same fate as what was primally repressed. Repression proper, therefore, is an after-pressure. (. . .) It is a mistake to emphasise only the repression which operates from the direction of the conscious upon that which is to be repressed; *quite as important is the attraction exercised by what was primally repressed upon everything with which it can establish a connection.*[27] (emphasis mine – M.D.)

Even before repression proper is fairly established, dreaming may occur; but such an experience does not count as what we usually call a dream, for at that stage there is no definable boundary yet in the unconscious separating dreams from the waking life. When repression proper becomes active, it interferes only with conscious processes of thought, recall and movement; it does not hinder "the instinctual representative from continuing to exist in the unconscious" – sometimes in

[27] Freud, 1915, "Repression", Standard Edition, vol. XIV.

their original form, but often transformed; it is the pressure of the repressed elements that leads the unconscious to seek release in dreams proper, which are "made for the recognition (. . .) of desire. (. . .) the elaboration of the dream is nourished by desire."[28] Dealing with dreams available for analysis, Freud identified the clue to the linguistic structure of the psychic region and discovered how this structure mediated between the unconscious and consciousness.

Lacan emphasizes this structure and elaborates on it following the model of Ferdinand de Saussure but changing the symbolic value of the "bar" devised by this major linguist. Every language (viewed as a linguistic structure) is built around a sign-system; the Saussurian model deployed this "bar" as a notational device in order to indicate that, though a particular pairing of a signifier (a "word-sound", the sound shape of a word) with a specific signified (a concept) is an arbitrary linkage, none the less this linkage (of the word-sound and the concept), as established in a given society, is in fact a secure combination – the signified has a strong bond with the signifier. Lacan, casting doubt on the security or strength of this bond, puts forward his characteristic example in which "what appears to be the same signified (a door) can be marked with two different signifiers 'Ladies' and 'Gentlemen' (. . .)", thus emphasizing the problem of reference. Wright reads Lacan as problematizing

> the process whereby parts of the world come to be referred to as things or persons. Illusion can enter the sign-system because the identification of the signified depends upon human judgments which can, notoriously and justifiably, differ. The Saussurian security is here removed; a hidden

---

[28] The value and validity of dream analysis are lucidly presented by Lacan, "Direction of treatment and principles of its power", op. cit., pp. 226-78.

> gap opens up between signifier and signified, the bar no longer a bond but a 'division'.[29]

Keeping in mind how this "division" is likely to operate in the unconscious which retains and employs the mechanism of "reversal" at its disposal since the pre-oedipal, pre-linguistic phase, we are now in a position to formulate effectively the place of Freud's concept of libido in his approach to metapsychology. Had the psychic region been truly all conscious, libido would not have had the properties it does. But the unconscious is indeed present, and has a major share in psychic – and consequently in social – events. Freud noted that

> The reversal affects only the *aims* of the instincts. The active aim (to torture, to look at) is replaced by the passive aim (to be tortured, to be looked at). Reversal of *content* is found in the single instance of the transformation of love into hate.[30]

What Freud describes as *content* in the above statement can be narrowed down to "affect". "Aims" involve "motility", which enables the subject to intervene in the external environment. We have already learned from Freud that, in the continuing contest for primacy over psychic processes that sets the stage for the emergence of the field known as the ego, the unconscious loses to consciousness in matters of motility, whereas affect is forever caught between pressures emanating from two opposing forces: the unconscious and a nascent conscious agency. Lacan conceives the field of contestation as a Möbius strip, where the encounter between the Imaginary and the Symbolic remains essentially ambiguous for constitutive reasons. The Imaginary sees the signifier one

---

[29] Wright, op. cit., p. 109. It will become evident as the discussion proceeds that illusion – in the sense of this passage – is not limited to a single identificatory moment.

[30] Freud, 1915, "Instincts", op. cit.

way, the Symbolic has a different view, and this duality has the effect of splitting the conscious from the unconscious.

Lacan's interpretation of the Freudian corpus thus proposes a certain identification between the forms of language and the psychic response to repression; accepting this hypothesis helps locate the self (ego) with its gender identity in its relatedness to parents and the world of objects. How can one love, given the realities of human language, without being either a "boy" or a "girl"?

> Language imposes a chain of words along which the ego must move while the unconscious remains in search of the object it has lost.[31]

In the Imaginary, the wish has always been inseparable from its fulfilment; immediate pleasure (presence) has been unquestioned. Desire *for* the mother and Desire *of* the mother have been one and the same. The Symbolic chain of language tries to substitute the Law of the Father for this Desire.

> The Father's words, those definitions out of which the object world is ready-made for the child (. . .) the object is not lost, but merely delayed – for how long in future time, he who is patient enough to learn to speak the Father's 'non' will discover.[32]

This is a "kind of trick", Wright goes on to say, creating the illusion that all is well under the Law of the Father. However, in the symbolic chain, the Mother, the child, their relationship, the place established for it in the world of others (humans, animals, objects), are all defined in terms of conventional language, every word of which stands for something (object) that is lost, lost to the Imaginary, associated with the baby/child who is no more. The worst loss apprehended (and ideally represented to the unconscious) is the loss of the body, its

---

31 Wright, op. cit., p. 111.

32 Ibid.

mutilation, resulting in a deep anxiety that Freud analysed as "castration anxiety". The fear of castration marks the growth of the mind, both in normal and in abnormal development. It is to the region of the lost child (who must be lost for the subject to meaningfully acquire the linguistic item "child") that psychoanalysis traces the origin of love, hate and of course ignorance.

It follows that love is literally and necessarily blind. The word "love", which in a certain sense stands for the loss of one's love (of the object), operates in the symbolic order of the human psyche in a way that cannot be grasped in terms of our ordinary understanding of language. It is by placing the Oedipus myth in this perspective that one begins to appreciate the significance of Freud's work on the Oedipus complex. I find the following quote helpful in the context of grappling with the problem. Jean Starobinski – an essayist and literary critic thoroughly conversant with psychoanalysis – is quoted by Anzieu as having made the following remark in 1970:

> The unconscious is not just language: it is dramaturgy, that is to say the staging of speech, spoken action (between the extremes of clamour and silence). *Oedipus Rex*, quintessential mythical drama, is instinct made visible in as pure a form as possible. Oedipus has no unconscious because he is our unconscious, by which I mean one of the essential roles that our wish has assumed. (. . .) It would be preposterous to attribute a psychology to him: he is already a psychical agency. (. . .) There is nothing behind Oedipus, because Oedipus is depth itself.[33]

Anzieu is critical of Lacan for failing to notice the "spoken action" character of the unconscious because of his overemphasis on the written form of language. There are reasons to believe that, on the question of the evolution of the

---

[33] Didier Anzieu, 1988, *Freud's Self-Analysis* (tr. Peter Graham), London: Hogarth Press and the Institute of Psycho-Analysis, pp. 244-45.

ego, Freud did become more and more favourable to a "structural" approach to the matter. In her introductory comments to Freud's *Ego and the Id* (1923), Anna Freud observes that in the 1920s Freud tried to integrate "two new insights gained in his analytic treatments" regarding the ego – which could no longer be viewed as exclusively conscious – and the unconscious, which appeared as "a characteristic of mental activity that can be found in every part of the psychic apparatus"; and that, as a result of his effort, "the earlier topographical model of psychic life was superseded by the structural model".[34] This fits in well with Lacan's structural emphasis.

But given the way Freud turns the myth of Oedipus into a category, its impact goes beyond the bare structurality of written language. This becomes evident if we take a closer look at his treatment of libido. Libido comes to stand for the sexual hunger (of the body) and not the stomach's hunger (for nourishment). At birth, through the period of infancy, the pleasure of the body and gratification through nourishment are inextricably linked. However, this fact, which had long been common knowledge, did not inspire Freud to write *Three Essays on Sexuality* in 1905. These essays emerged out of the insight gained through his study and observations of irregularities and failures in the sexual and general behaviour of adults. Described as "a quantitatively variable force which could serve as a measure of processes and transformations occurring in the field of sexual excitation", libido was distinguished by Freud in respect of its special origin from

---

[34] Freud, 1986, *The Essentials of Psychoanalysis: Selected with an Introduction and Commentaries by Anna Freud* (tr. James Strachey), London: Hogarth, pp. 435-37. These insights led him to remark that the ego is not to be taken as entirely coinciding with the system Cs [Conscious], for "it has distinct unconscious parts". Second, the concept of the Unconscious now came to be restricted to "a quality of psychic process, i.e. to a characteristic that can be found in every part of the psychic apparatus".

the general energy. He also postulated qualitative characteristics distinguishing "ego-libido" from "object-libido". Ego-libido (also described as narcissistic libido) was viewed as

> the great reservoir from which the object cathexes are sent out and into which they are withdrawn once more; the narcissistic libidinal cathexis of the ego is the original state of things, realised in earliest childhood, and is merely covered by the later extrusions of libido, but in essentials persists behind them.[35]

Transformations of the object-libido are observable, but "ego-libido and other forms of energy operating in the ego" can scarcely be distinguished in and through these transformations. So even though he bifurcated libido into two types, Freud's understanding of libidinal transformations was restricted to object-libido. Object-libido takes on an object; during puberty, the object-choice from the psychical side and the physiological preparations for it can be seen as two processes converging on a single aim (the new sexual aim). But this is not the beginning of the operation of libido. "It was Freud's merit that in the creation of his libido concept he welded together somatic and psychic processes into an inseparable unit", observes Anna Freud. This was accomplished in two moves: (i) Freud separated sexuality from its reproductive connotation, relegating the latter to a secondary position; (ii) deciding to consider "those merely affectionate and friendly impulses to which usage applies the exceedingly ambiguous word 'love'" as included in libidinal impulses, Freud extended the term libido in both directions and had no compunction about asserting that "The finding of an object is in fact a refinding of it".[36] The subject facing puberty appears to make a fresh object

---

[35] Freud, 1905, "Three Essays on the Theory of Sexuality", Standard Edition, vol. VII.

[36] Freud, 1905, op. cit.

choice; but his first object choice was made in infancy and was lost, after which the subject became auto-erotic (i.e. the object-libido withdrew into the ego-libido); when the fresh object choice occurs, due to internal and external (physiological) pressures, there is in fact a resurgence of the first object choice. However, in our everyday life, our common sense speaks of love and friendship in the context of fresh object choices that the conscious mind does not recognize as a resurgence of an older choice. Our conscious experiences from puberty onwards belong, in fact, to the middle phase of a process whose beginning and end are equally unknown to us. Freud, proposing a theory based on empirical material, shows us a way to reconstruct the beginning, taking as a point of departure the fact that anxiety marks the transformation of the "original affect into a qualitatively different affect" – diving deep in the dark corners of our psychic life lost and forgotten.

How can a fuller knowledge of that life be acquired and adequately communicated? Here I would remember Kaplan:

> An epistemology which takes account of the depth psychology of Freud and his successors is yet to be written.[37]

---

[37] Kaplan, op. cit., pp. 130-31.

2

The Indian Context of Love and Friendship

WE do not have the resources to ascertain the validity of the claim that

> the organisation of the Sangha in the Buddha's lifetime was not, it would seem, the mere child of necessity. The Triratna was already conceived as a unit, for the Buddha said in terms [*sic*] that after his passing the Dhamma was to be the disciples' Teacher, and the Sangha was founded as a missionary enterprise within a few weeks of the Enlightenment.[1]

In any case, this claim about the *triratna* (the Buddha, the Sangha and the Dhamma) as "a unit" has no direct bearing on our study. We are asking a different question: what sense does it make that Buddha, who alone among the prophets untiringly emphasized the need for his disciples to cultivate the virtues of perfect self-reliance and responsibility,[2] trusted

---

[1] Christmas Humphreys, 1951, *Buddhism*, Harmondsworth: Penguin, 3rd edn. repr. 1967, p. 132.

[2] Like many other scholars, Abraham Kaplan highlights "a recurrent theme in the Buddha's discourses and sermons"; it is one of the last injunctions that Buddha gave his disciples when he was dying: "Be lamps unto yourselves; hold fast as a refuge to the truth; look not for refuge to anyone besides yourselves. Not even to Gautama the Buddha". Abraham Kaplan, 1961, *The New World of Philosophy*, New York: Vintage, p. 244.

the efficacy of the Sangha, an institution? How are we to visualize a perfectly self-reliant and responsible individual situated in a Sangha? There seems to be some discrepancy between the image of a person embedded in an institution and the virtues of self-reliance and self-actualization. And yet perhaps a link between the two ideals can be forged along the following lines.

The chains that bind human creatures to the transitory world of suffering are embedded in Desire. To release oneself, one has to take a deep and careful look at these chains, as Gautama the Buddha had himself done. In his search for a solution to the riddle of human existential suffering, he approached learned sages, who gave him their affection and blessings, but not the answers he was looking for. He took to penance and severe austerity, which brought him very close to death, but the object remained as elusive as ever. Giving up austerity and recalling his childhood experience of first ever true serenity under a tree in the presence of his father working in the field, he sat down after having his meal (obtained by begging) and meditated. In the course of this effort "Desire", personified as Māras/demons, distracted him until he could look evil in the eye and emerge enlightened. The mark of his final victory in acquiring enlightenment was manifested in his serene, *compassionate* (not *dispassionate* or cold) acceptance of the presence of Sujata with a bowl of delicious food which she had brought as an offering to her deity. He was not begging; this time, the food came as a pleasant offering. The Buddha's acceptance of this food stands for his readiness to accept life *but on his own terms*. Life is full of peril and suffering, and the greatest danger is that it appears pleasant and attractive. The primal source of suffering lies in the transitoriness of all that is beautiful and pleasurable. If "Desire" could be switched off, then the transitory would stop luring the individual.

Switching desire off does not put an end to the world with its transitoriness, but the world ceases to pose a threat to the individual. How is the individual free from the trammels of desire constituted? Under normal circumstances, desire is intimately interwoven with ordinary human actions. Does the vanquishing of desire transform active individuals into inactive sites of mere presence? This question, posed at the level of the true meaning of what Freud famously called the "*nirvāṇa* principle", has led to long and significant discussions in the past, and will do so in times to come. But in the context of our inquiry I propose an approach that links the image of the individual who has vanquished desire with the concept of the Sangha.

The removal of desire has to be followed by immediately instituting some psychic agency which urges individuals to act and in this sense replaces desire. Buddha's enlightenment gave him access to methods of replacing passion-laden desire with rational perception, through the careful cultivation of the commonality of one individual's interests with others in the world of action. What Freud enunciated as a motto much later in human history was personally accomplished by Buddha; in him, rational compassion (the ego) reigned supreme over the psychic region where passion (the id) had been the only force. It is this achievement that is celebrated in the idea of the Sangha, a cultural entity that stands in support of enlightened individuals rising above their natural dispositions. In this way, individuals participating in enlightenment are intrinsically *constituted as the Sangha* at the level of their definitional, essential action, which eliminates the apparent opposition between the notion of self-reliant personal responsibility and institutionality. The gathering of individuals-in-the-Sangha has nothing to do with the coercive cohesion that other social institutions impose.

Before we move into the discussion of power (coercion), I wish to emphasize a basic difference between Buddha's conception of suffering and Freudian notions of (or more specifically Freud's own formulations of) the pleasure principle that construe "pain" as absence of "pleasure". For Buddha, suffering (though removable by persistent personal effort) is a human condition, a metaphysical category not responsive to the impact of possible social change. In Buddha's view, human childhood and its conflicts have no bearing on the original shape or the distortions of psychic representations of desire. For Freud, infancy and childhood are crucial. This is why it is possible to evolve agendas for the reconstruction of the family or of society on the basis of Freud's ideas, whereas Buddha offers personal prescriptions for self-improvement to every child and every adult on an equal footing without regard to how a given person is embedded in social structures. His identification of the root of all malaise, however, remains strikingly similar to what Freud was to discover towards the end of the nineteenth century – by which I mean the *Mother*. It is a crucial act on the compassionate Buddha's part to efface the Mother from the order of the Sangha, disregarding the traditional Indian priorities that committed all individuals, even sages and ascetics, to a universal position of submission to the Mother. Satyavatī's command was sufficient to make Vyāsa beget descendants for Vicitravīrya through the latter's (unwilling) widows.[3] Buddha reversed this priority when Mahāprajāpati Gotamī was made to surrender completely to the Sangha before she was accepted for admission in the order.

When Śaṅkarācārya reaffirmed the primacy of the Vedic Hindu tradition, retrieving the terrain of faith that had been lost to Buddhism, he restored the Mother to her original place of pride and unquestioned respectworthiness.[4] Śaṅkara's

---

[3] Iravati Karve, 1974, *Yuganta: The End of an Epoch,* Bombay: Sangam Books, pp. 14-15. Karve, of course, involves Bhīṣma in the decision-making process.

[4] Swami Apurbananda, *Acharya Sankar*, Calcutta: Udbodhan Karyalaya, 3rd edn. 1383 BE [CE 1976].

denunciation of the woman and his glorification of the mother manifests a split characteristic of the Indian psyche that merits elaborate study elsewhere. What I focus on here is of limited import and is simply this: Buddha can be viewed as the one who located the principle of deep passion in Desire-for/of-the-Mother and who thus concluded that the mother must be made to surrender all claims of primacy over the subject (more precisely, over the subject's action, for recall that Buddha would not admit the reality of the subject independent of the action); Mahāprajāpati's surrender symbolized the surrender of desire's claim of primacy over the subject's conscious cultural activity.

But the realization of the primacy of conscious action (or, in non-Buddhist terms, of the self) is not something that one can receive as a gift from others; each individual has to attain this realization through personal effort on their own. One must be one's own light when one is resisting the evil lures of passion. However, how can one tell if one has made some headway, or measure how much one has achieved? Buddha knew he had succeeded when Sujātā appeared with delicacies on her platter, seeing that she had come not to distract him but to acknowledge the enlightened one as a deity – compressing what needs to be said about Sujātā's perception and Buddha's grasp of this perception, I am using "deity" here to refer to the fact that Buddha had freed himself from bondage to the human life cycle. Now, others who were trying to follow Buddha's example would need testing criteria and competent witnesses who could help the seekers to apply them; one purpose of the Sangha was to make these available. Men who had similar ideas, similar efforts and similar aims, brought together, provided "each to each a looking-glass". This remark is of course purely speculative – Buddha and his companions left no documents indicating their reasons for the course of action that led to the setting up of the Sangha. From anecdotal written accounts, however, we can surmise that he followed a method of direct democracy in matters of discipline within the Sangha. This information is significant in so far as it lends support to our thesis that *friendship*, institutionalized in the Buddhist Sangha (which was explicitly designed for the cultivation of *metta-bhāvanā*, friendly cogitation) to a degree not seen in any earlier institution, *is a relation between equals*; as a state of mind, it is free from passion (strong attachments of love and hostility), full of *consideration* for the friend in particular and *human concern* in general. This state of mind does not tend to emerge spontaneously; a truly friendly person is very uncommon and rare to come by.

General human concern as Buddha understood it consisted in the preservation of life and the alleviation of pain (through cessation of worldly desire in the subject and personal care for "others"). The stories and anecdotes told and retold in connection with Buddha's enlightenment and teaching emphasize his "caring". That he spoke to others clearly and persuasively is not surprising, for such a prince would have been trained in various arts, including that of public speaking. But his "caring" was distinctly his *own*, and had to do with his notion of the essence of human situatedness in this life. This notion is illustrated in various narratives. The Jātaka story of Vāsavadattā and Upagupta (a disciple of Buddha's) has been retold by Tagore in a poem that makes the point that, to a body denuded of its power and attraction, compassion alone can offer the truly human touch and support that it needs. The courtesan Vāsavadattā was refused by this disciple of Buddha's, Upagupta, when she approached him physically. Tagore's poetic version has Upagupta promise her that he will return when the time comes. The appointed hour comes when she falls ill with smallpox, whereupon the community entertained for years by her charming presence banishes her from the locality. There is no irony that this tragic hour of the courtesan's fall should be the "appointed hour" of tryst with Upagupta; the point of the story is that the human body is given to us to be cared for by *karuṇā*, by human compassion.

It can be argued that it is in pain and misery that all living creatures are one, and that in times of pleasure they assert their individual identity through communication and companionship with the select few. Buddha aimed to remove pain but not to replace it with pleasure or happiness. The object of his quest was *nirveda* (detachment), the goal he suggested for his true disciples as well. The imagination of our times finds it natural to ask: how can "detachment" possibly form a basis for friendship?

To such a question, we can imagine a counter-question from the viewpoint of Buddha, the compassionate: How could ego-centred attachment possibly promote friendship? No authentic friendship can be sustained among persons who are in that state, for attachment deeply involves the ego. As Aristotle has argued at length, although friendship can be imagined as developing at various levels of mutuality of action, true friendship becomes sustainable only when two good persons are drawn to each other entirely by virtue of their purity of heart and not to complement each other at the level of individual deficiencies, instrumental usefulness, etc.[5] Scholars have noted that the true spirit of the Sangha was vitiated by inner factions even before Buddha's death.[6] This fact merely highlights the problem of dissociating compassion from passion – friendship from love. We keep this complex issue (to which we shall return) pending for the moment, and note those principles invoked by Buddha in his lifetime that amount to a social philosophy. He was anti-establishment,

---

[5] Aristotle, 1926, *Nicomachean Ethics*, ed. E. Capps et al., tr. H. Rackham, London/New York: Loeb Classical Library.

[6] Amulya Chandra Sen, 1965, *Buddhakatha*, Calcutta: Bharat Vidya Vihar.

having rejected the traditional authority of his royal lineage and also of the Vedic scriptures; he was eager to initiate a mobile brotherhood of friends. As a sincere believer in the method of friendly persuasion, he never coerced any disciple into obedience by external threats; he was a thorough rationalist who could see passion in its true colours. Buddha's rationalism did not take the form of theoretical systematization; his chief aim was the practical use of reason. From the texts recording his discourses and preaching, any enthusiastic and thoughtful disciple could have gleaned something that would retrospectively count as an Indian social philosophy – a possibility that was not realized until the *Bhagavad-Gītā* was composed, with a different world-view, in the form of a dialogue between two friends, Kr̥ṣṇa and Arjuna.

On our way to examining that dialogue with some care, we need to slightly enlarge the scope of our scrutiny by raising questions that have often been neglected in this context.

Stories thematizing friendship in religious texts as well as in the secular or folk traditions revolve around male protagonists. Images of women with female friends are rarely highlighted in the Indian tales and legends we are familiar with. Ordinary observation, however, suggests that – despite the rarity of true friendship in these as in other circles – bonds of mutual friendship among women exist and are strong. If we speak in terms of the traditional division of the Indian household into the interior zone and the outer house and courtyard, there has never been any reason for believing that those inhabiting the *antaḥpura* (the interior zone) were any less capable of forming and sustaining bonds of serious friendship than those who spend their day in the outer house. However, the reality and importance of this capability has often been obscured by a persistent myth about the "interior" and its inhabitants. As this myth would have it, the "interior" stands for darkness, for the prevention of free mobility, for suppression, and also for all that is petty, sordid, inconsequential. This myth may be seen as an exteriorization of a deeply felt psychic duality (unconscious vs. conscious, forces of darkness and inaccessibility vs. those of light and open communicability) that leads us in our conscious lives to tend to reject or deny (repress) the inner while extolling the outer arena. However, in places where well-built structures of authority are not in place (e.g. in mobile groups, village complexes depending on a single water resource such as a river, or even organized groups in the middle of a crisis), people inhabiting the "interior" (i.e. women) are found together in close, friendly contact offering warmth and succour to one another. One can catch a glimpse of this community of women through oral traditions embodied in folk tales and rhymes, semi-religious local rituals and prayers intended to bring about prosperity and welfare for people in general and for children in particular, as well as through the continuation of "wifely" performances on auspicious occasions like marriage. Written and recorded documents have always – as they do now – spoken of women in their relatedness to men, either adding to their glory or bringing about their downfall. As a result, one hears of Guhaka and Rāma's useful and warm friendship in an episodic passage within the *Rāmāyaṇa*, but one is given no access to the relationships that Sītā must have formed with the women of Rāvaṇa's *antaḥpura*, his "interior", which must have helped her to keep her spirit intact through the dark days of imprisonment. That Vibhīṣaṇa's wife was an unequal but well-meaning friend of Sītā's is a fact that readers in India often associate exclusively with the mutation of the narrative in its modern retelling by Michael Madhusudan Dutt in his *Meghnād-badh* (The Slaying of Meghanāda) – not with the "real" *Rāmāyaṇa*. And yet even in the narrative of the "real" *Rāmāyaṇa*, the women in Ayodhyā, notwithstanding the presence of a conspiratorial Mantharā and a self-seeking Kaikeyī, apparently continued to live in harmony in Rāma's absence without much ado. This harmonious coexistence that women are capable of does not become salient in written documents, because the "interior", like the unconscious, is seen only through the turmoil it produces once in a while in its effort to control and manipulate the outer region, which acquires its primacy through its contact with the world of the "real" – populated by institutions, groups and cultures. One may speculate that the Indian people (like all the others) experienced less repression and more freedom within and outside their household in the era before they evolved the codes that defined societal structures. Under the codified rules of civilized society, rationality and the irrational could no longer coexist in a state of overlap. The outer house had to count as out of bounds for the denizens of the "interior". And yet the multicultural societal frame that was India possibly did find a way to retain its polymorphous character, so that even at the time when the power of words was established, dreams were not effectively separated from action.[7] Buddha's enlightened rationalism saw through the ambiguity of it all and, by setting up an order of friendship where the mother qua "Mother" had no right of entry, he aimed to put in place a perfect division between the world of dreams and that of conscious utterances in public. The "Mother" in India stood for the idea of uncorrupting and incorruptible (passionate) love providing succour and strength to the individual. By rejecting this idea, Buddha robbed Indian women of their distinctive value, which left their self-image in disarray. This is of some importance in the context of our investigation of love and friendship.

The southern part of the Indian subcontinent, with old traditions characterized by texts and tales in large part distinct

---

[7] A stimulating analysis on this point is available in Wendy Doniger O'Flaherty, 1984, *Dreams, Illusion, and Other Realities*, Chicago: University of Chicago Press; Indian Edition: Motilal Banarsidass, Delhi, 1987.

from the north, retained this difference throughout much of India's recorded social history. Thus, it is no wonder that Śaṅkarācārya, with his pronounced devotion for the Mother, should hail from the south. What the south stands for, institutionally speaking, is no Aristotelian "community" providing "the essence of friendship". A community structured in terms of power and status goes about its business, and within this business certain individuals "happen" to make friends, coincidentally. Afterwards, such friendships are tested, and some friends turn out to be true friends. There is nothing wrong, of course, or nothing striking, about tales depicting such friendship: the pattern is obviously not specific to southern India. In general, both in ancient and in contemporary India, recorded accounts of friendship developing over a variegated range of social contexts are seldom found. Older texts on the whole express the idea that he who is available in times of crisis – such as being summoned to the court or to the cremation ground – is a friend.[8] An extensive treatise on *Anaṅga-Raṅga*, the art of love, provides resources for improving one's grasp of the subtleties of man–woman relationships; but there are none that address the human relation known as friendship. A careful look at the *Tirukkural* would, I believe, confirm my contention. This classic – I have been given to understand – forms the basis for the

---

[8] I wondered if this point of view was perhaps too utilitarian to have originated in authentic Indian contexts where idealism has been prevalent for millennia. However, the major Sanskritist Dr Sukumari Bhattacharya dispelled my doubts as to its authenticity. She mentioned many other Sanskrit aphorisms of practical wisdom that have been handed down over the centuries but that cannot be attributed to any specific theoretical system of social or religious thinking. Kauṭilya's *Arthaśāstra* is, of course, known for its emphasis on instrumental and diplomatic considerations. In this connection, reference may be made to A.L. Basham's *The Wonder that was India*, London: Sidgwick & Jackson, 1954, 3rd edn. 1967, Rupa Paperback 1981, p. 80.

general ethos and the social mores of much of southern India. The text provides a remarkable formulation of what the good life is about, of social and institutional issues, in the context of discussing not some theological heaven but *life in this world*.[9] Now, even such a major work offers serious analyses of "the good" and of "love" – however, no analysis of friendship. Its world-view has no place for friendship as a value.

The quest for narrative representations of friendship is somewhat less frustrating. Instances of friendship are found in both Vaiṣṇava and non-Vaiṣṇava literary traditions. When a young man in love looks for a confidant, some friend whom circumstances happen to have placed near him comes to his aid. This can happen to a young woman as well. In narratives of this type – regardless of gender – the friendship tends to arise between social unequals and stays focused on finding a quick solution to the problem that lover is facing. After the lovers are safely united, nothing much is heard about the friend, unless he or she comes to be entangled in yet another relationship of love – a story within a story. Daṇḍin's *Daśa-Kumāra-Carita*[10] illustrates the latter type of narrative. However, that text should not be seen merely as an instance of the type – it has distinctive qualities of its own that merit attention. In the first place, the story does not begin with a simple statement such as "they happened to be near each other": ten princes cannot just "happen" to become friends through chance proximity at some fortuitous moment. The king, who is the father of Prince Rājavāhana – the hero of the story, constant through all its subplots – assembles nine other boys whose friendship he seeks for his son. Those other boys are princes

9 Subramania Gopalan, 1979, *The Social Philosophy of Tirukkural*, Delhi: Affiliated East-West Press.

10 Daṇḍin, *Daśa-Kumāra-Carita: The Ten Princes*, tr. with an introduction by Arthur W. Ryder, Chicago: University of Chicago Press, 1927; Indian Edition: Delhi: Jaico, 1956.

as well, "all destined in the sequel to royalty". This book – written in Sanskrit prose around the seventh century CE – was intended to amuse cultivated readers, not to preach moral lessons. Its characters make their way through many expeditions and adventures, at the end of which every friend eventually finds all the others, and there is a joyful reunion of friends. The king and Rājavāhana's mother bless them; each goes to his destined place, with the bride he has chosen to accept the responsibility of a kingdom.

Within the twists of the narrative the reader encounters love, hate, conspiracy, self-effacing loyalty, generosity, deception, magic, devotion, the power of gods, of destiny. What is striking, above all, is the way Prince Rājavāhana responds to the account of ordeals and final success that each friend narrates before declaring loyalty to Rājavāhana – before promising to support him in all his future projects. Rājavāhana suspends critical judgement and with unreserved cordiality accepts all that is said to him, congratulating each friend for his achievements. If we choose to identify this attitude of unreserved approval as the core of friendship, we must note at the same time that, as a term indicating mutual relatedness, *friendship* operates in this narrative through the projects of these mutually related individuals who are trying to demonstrate their valour and competence as men of action.

The passages in the *Daśa-Kumāra-Carita* that portray intense *love* between princes and princesses describe love as an overwhelming emotion that leaves the heroes *powerless* until the women who have aroused this strong passion provide the antidote, using their own *power* – of counselling and reassurance – to restore the heroes' spirits. However, the beloved maidens themselves are sometimes a little too young and timid to realize and deploy their own power. Friendly men and women, willing to mediate, come to the rescue of our heroes, finding the right resources to restore them to their full capacity for glory. Parents who help by bringing friends together, such as Rājavāhana's parents, manifest the wisdom that grows around the realization that life's pleasures and pains can be experienced with poise and courage only thanks to one's friends. Without friends, the enterprise called life appears dry and colourless.

This last observation becomes particularly significant when we notice that narratives of friendship are all stories of the young. Infancy, like old age, is no time for making friends. This does not hold of love. Consider, for instance, a typical philosophical statement such as:

> It is not for the love of all that all is dear but for the love of the soul in all that all is dear.[11]

The soul, however, is not believed in any theological doctrine to emerge in youth and to disappear before the infirmity of old-age prevails, crippling the capacity of human beings to stand related to others. On the contrary, the soul is present as much during infancy as in old age, and moves into another form after taking its leave from the dead body. If love is about the soul, love is ageless.

To see the contrast more concretely, it is best to take a closer look at exemplary narratives. In the case of most vividly portrayed friendship in the Indian tradition – that between Kṛṣṇa and Arjuna – we find the relationship being forged in the course of Arjuna's youthful escapades (e.g. his abduction of the Yādava maiden Subhadrā). Before that phase, Arjuna knew Kṛṣṇa only as a kinsman; as a powerful Yādava and a relative of Kuntī (the mother of the Pāṇḍavas), Kṛṣṇa could be counted on as a *potential* ally; but Arjuna's adventures brought about a new closeness between Kṛṣṇa and this unique Pāṇḍava.

---

[11] *The Upaniṣads*, tr. with an introduction by Juan Mascaró, Harmondsworth: Penguin, 1965. My reference is to the selection from the *Bṛhadāraṇyaka*, specifically to p. 131.

Kṛṣṇa's project on earth was to save the world from perpetrators of evil; so he responded to Arjuna's friendly overtures with warmth; mutual friendship developed between the two. When we set this account of the beginnings of their friendship over against the standard account of the love of Rādhā and Kṛṣṇa, we find confirmation of what was observed above about the difference between friendship and love.

There are several versions of the Rādhā–Kṛṣṇa story. When we quickly consider three variants – in which Rādhā is portrayed:

1. as older than Kṛṣṇa, already married;
2. as born with congenital blindness, destined to be cured when the boy Kṛṣṇa touches her eyes;
3. as an adolescent unaware of the harm that the overwhelming passion of love could inflict on her when her first encounter with the boy Kṛṣṇa charms her –

We find that what varies is Rādhā's place in the story. Kṛṣṇa, on the other hand, is consistently portrayed as a sylvan lad, playful and musical, carefully protected by his foster-mother until he eventually grows into late adolescence, ready to leave Vrindavan and fulfil his mission. At the appointed time, Akrūra comes to fetch him, and Kṛṣṇa leaves his mother and his childhood companions including Rādhā, to recover his father's kingdom from the evil clutches of Kaṁsa. Until that moment of departure, neither Kṛṣṇa nor Rādhā pursues any independent plan of action: their only project is "love". Love leads nowhere; it simply *is*. When its time is over in one phase, it is transformed into something else (e.g. energy for action, for new plans, for new experiences); this is what we witness when Kṛṣṇa emerges as a leader of his people. In the course of this later development, his love, Rādhā, disappears from the realm of his body or, in other words, returns to his ego/self. The simple content of this enduring love-story has been subjected to excellent religious and metaphysical interpretations and literary representations. By all accounts, Rādhā becomes *eternal* through her disappearance. This is not just about Rādhā; it is appropriate to describe love itself in these terms. Love's eternity owes its origin to its disappearance. Since love cannot be located anywhere in particular, its presence is felt everywhere.

Unlike love, friendship is a situated phenomenon. Projects emerge differently in different phases of development; correspondingly, the location of friendship keeps moving. A childhood playmate retains a certain nostalgic value for the individual; but new engagements in life call for the formation of fresh circles of friends. As long as individuals are capable of rising to this challenge, they can revive or renew their friendship, carrying over the full colour and verve of the older phase of the relationship. New friends can be, and sometimes are, introduced to one's older friends, to form a bigger social group of common friends. This is not an option available in the case of love, an exclusive, very personal type of bond. A loving couple speaks a language that is more of a "private language" than a single person in his isolated world of thought could ever fashion. It is this quality of privacy, and its loss, that make the story of Rāma and Sītā in the *Rāmāyaṇa* poignant and tragic.

The central story of that epic begins to take shape when King Daśaratha's private promise to his beloved queen Kaikeyī is transformed into a public event – the banishment of crown prince Rāma from the kingdom; the overall structure of the narrative derives its coherence through the private inseparability of Rāma and Sītā in love which comes under attack from external forces. Rāma's war with Rāvaṇa is a celebration of the individual's effort to protect the tenderness of privacy from public intrusion and disgrace. The *Mahābhārata*, on the other hand, weaves the story of public life and heroism. We find friends and enemies there, but hardly any "privacy" in the sense of this discussion, apart from Kuntī's hidden yearning for her long-lost first-born, with whom we find her pleading in secret. Spurning the gift of mother's love that she offers, Karṇa says:

> you have committed the sin of destroying my name and fame. Even though born a Kshatriya, I did not receive the sacrament of a Kshatriya. What enemy could do me a greater wrong? (. . .) The mother in you was dead then.[12]

One understands Kuntī's secret better by tracing it back to her *curiosity* to see how the magical power of invocation works. It is the satisfaction of this urge that causes her first male child to arrive before she is ready to receive and retain her baby. He remains, in consequence, a threat to her public image, and a passion in private. This part-episode has the potency of "myth" but has been excluded from the core of the *Mahābhārata*'s structure; the epic defuses all private tensions in public action in full view, involving open strife and taking sides among the contending powers. The sacred text of the *Bhagavad-Gītā* with its social philosophy can be read effectively against this background of the attempt to transform deep passion into social power. This process is evidently very different from the process of *metta* initiated by Buddha.

Buddha offered serenity with compassion for all who suffer an identical fate of deprivation (another name for which is *dukkha*, and whose origins lie in *tanha*) – a serenity and a compassion attainable through rational enlightenment. But Kṛṣṇa in the *Gītā* opens up three distinct symbolic orders, offering:

1. total sublimation through reason and the power of knowledge;

[12] Karve, op. cit.

2. action in the proper spirit in terms of roles prescribed by birth plus inborn qualities;
3. a complete surrender of the search for a human answer to the riddle of human existence with its inherent contradictions, and a decision to dedicate oneself in emotive devotion to the deity.

While this is a very different space of choices, there is however one shared primary lesson offered by both the teachers – the compassionate Buddha and the divine charioteer Kṛṣṇa – namely, the point that nothing can possibly be known about the beginning and the end of the drama of an individual life on the earth. Within the frame of ordinary human experience, the middle of the play is all that one can know and deal with. Beyond this significant observation on the limits of human intellect and comprehension, Buddha's core teachings and those of the *Gītā* had very little in common. Was it the sharp divergence of their approaches to the course of action open to human beings caught in this only partly intelligible context that led so many insightful and learned scholars to stop short of working out a comprehensive social philosophy for India, a philosophy that might have brought these trends of thought and discourse closer – testing them against each other? This is no place to pursue such a question, which goes well beyond the scope of this study. We restrict ourselves to the consideration of a few points of immediate relevance to our work.

We have already noted that Buddha emphasized reason; his notion of the enlightened individual (as exemplified by his actions after attaining *bodhi*) was one of a perfectly rational identity extending a consciously cultivated "loving kindness" to all Others. The Other, perceived as "other" but not as a threat, presents an opportunity for affirming one's compassion. Through his silence about the question as to whether there is any common thread (such as would be made available by the idea of a god or a *Brahman*) binding the "Other" to the self or the subject in a systematic way, Buddha emphasized rational and secular individuality. The individual continues to undertake "action" – either with full awareness and control, a mode that does not bind the performer to the performance, or in ignorance, which entangles the two in a confused half-understanding that gets in the way of a full and lucid awareness of what performance is all about. Ending this confused entanglement is the goal, not the termination of all effort but the termination of what our ordinary confused understanding takes to be the essence of effort.

The metaphysical foundations of Buddha's notion of action and the sāṁsāric cycle, coupled with his silence about the idea of self, present a problem which is not amenable to any easy solution. Kaplan compares this silent (and in some passages not so silent) rejection of "the notion of a substantial self providing an enduring basis for self-identity" with Bertrand Russell's position among contemporary western thinkers and to that of "David Hume, the father of modern empiricism".[13] This comparison leaves us clueless as to how the notion of *karma* (action) accepted by Buddha could be blended with the notion of a non-enduring actor (self) in a consistent philosophical understanding. This emphasis on "action going beyond the limits of the lifespan of its individual performer" is also present in the *Bhagavad-Gītā*. The *Gītā* with its rich metaphorical architecture casts the performer as an actor on a given stage with a given role whose rules are entirely beyond the actor's control, for he has had no voice in their formulation. If his search for self-knowledge provides him with a clue to the meaning of it all, he will come to terms with the fact that he does not, by virtue of being an actor or performer, have

[13] Kaplan, op. cit. Reference may also be made to: *The Buddhist Tradition in India, China and Japan*, ed. William Theodore de Bary, New York: Modern Library, 1969; New York: Vintage edn., 1972.

any right or power to go beyond the limits of performing his actions; he will also come to realize that this "*being* an actor" is not a genuine selfhood. The genuine, real self within him is none other than the absolute *Brahman*; the visible stagecraft is His pleasure; it conforms to no principle of necessity that human perception is able to recognize. Now, this absolutistic notion – in terms of which the truth of individuality lies in the rejection of the empirical self as spurious and the assertion of non-identity – does not fit well with Buddha's social ideal of friendship and personal care.

This conclusion is difficult to reconcile with the "Advaitin" assertion, by Ramchandra Gandhi, that our "central nervous system in its secret nature" has "the power of awakening self to self-knowledge, to the knowledge of oneness with all that is and thus flood it with unanxiousness. Not only in the Jñānī fully self-realised, Yājñavalkya and Buddha, Christ and Ramaṇa, but in all of us the central nervous system harbours this power (. . .)."[14] I am not considering issues regarding "the deepest power of the central nervous system" or about man's essential character in the context of Buddha's inquiry, for these were not issues Buddha raised either. His concern was the alleviation of human suffering, not theorization about essential human nature. It is entirely conceivable that the human essence in its wisdom does not care about social structure. In that case, it is unconcerned with friendship as we understand it.

A framework that valorises love in its serious purity, and at the same time enjoins one to regard *everybody* as oneself on the basis of a deeper notion of the *self*, is intended to lead to the realization that self-love encompasses love for all – whereupon love shall prevail in its pure, abstract, universal form. But the kind of friendship celebrated in Buddha's

---

[14] Ramchandra Gandhi, 1984, *I am Thou: Meditations on the Truth of India*, Pune: Indian Philosophical Quarterly Publications, p. 142.

teaching and practice respects the friend's individuality, his freedom to "be his own light". Humphreys says of Buddhist culture:

> (. . .) always it fought against caste; (. . .) and the value placed upon the individual has always gone hand-in-hand with a remarkable tolerance.[15]

This culture with its focus on the individual at the empirical level retains its distinctiveness, which comes out clearly when we place it side by side with the culture nurtured by the *Bhagavad-Gītā*.

The theory of disinterested action is indeed common to the Buddhist tradition and the *Gītā*'s teaching; however, when Buddha speaks of disinterested action, by "disinterested" he means "not attaching oneself emotionally" and "having no ulterior motive for gain"; but the compassionate one acts for the preservation of life and alleviation of pain; this looks like "action with definite ends in view" from the standpoint of the teachings of the *Gītā*. An action performed *with a view to bringing about a foreseen end* makes it an interested action in terms of that standpoint, which insists that the performer of truly "disinterested" actions should have no end in mind other than *scrupulously exact enactment of the performance*. The *Gītā* also emphasizes that, in terms of absolute reality, the living and the dead, the victor and the vanquished are coexistent, equally non-existent, for all this differentiation and colourful multiform creation is nothing but a world of appearance manifesting the overflowing pleasure (which by the same token is also the power) of Kṛṣṇa, the only true *being*. But Buddha, who maintains a consistent silence on matters theological, thereby refuses to reduce the world of multiplicity to a unique being, to a *puruṣa*, to a Kṛṣṇa. In other words, the notion of *māyā* – better translated in this context as "overflowing pleasure"

[15] Humphreys, 1951, op. cit.

than as "illusion" – increases the distance between Buddha's thinking and the *Gītā*. For a comprehensive social philosophy to emerge in ancient India that would bridge such a gap and subsume both these traditions was thus out of the question.

The difficulty was all the more aggravated by the *Gītā*'s teaching about the efficacy of *bhakti* (emotive devotion) as a way of life conducive to true liberation. This alternative provided a rationale for a complete surrender of one's right to make decisions, one's responsibility for making decisions – a surrender that suits the majority of men and women, not only here in India, but virtually all over the world. Self-reliance and responsibility need to be acquired through rigorous self-discipline, as Buddha has rightly observed. The way of emotive devotion – which permitted a release of tension by means of complete surrender to God, whose loving presence was to be intuitively felt through ecstasy – helped bring infantile love back to the social plane of action. This shift totally defeated the purpose of Buddha's teaching in India, and made it impossible for the idea of friendship to develop further in that phase of history. In its later stages, Buddhism turned to metaphysics and developed into a "religion" offering succour for spiritual hunger – retaining as much of its distinctiveness as possible within the fold of a religious movement. This process allowed Indian society to take its course away from Buddha's anti-authoritarian world-view that had placed the individual at the centre. The majority in India, under the impact of the *Bhagavad-Gītā*'s vision, gave Buddha a position of honour and pride, including him in the Hindu family of gods as an *avatāra* of Viṣṇu. This was in perfect consistency with the attitude of emotive devotion which had prevailed, and whose effect on the Indian idea of love we are about to take up for study.

Did *bhakti* as a notion admit any references to the physical? This is not an easy question to answer empirically. It is possible that the impact of *bhakti* produced a few cracks in the orthodoxy of Indian philosophical thinking long before the appearance of Śaṅkara. In the event, Śaṅkara was the author who restored the balance of ideas in favour of the traditional Hindu world-view accepting the Vedas. He presented this world-view not in terms of blind faith but on the basis of his superb use of logical argumentation, proposing to keep the physical, "perishable" order and the metaphysical, "real" order separate and yet deeply connected. The emergence of this world-view, and of Śaṅkara as its exponent, needs to be contextualized in relation to earlier historical events which shaped the social mood in India from CE 300 onwards.

From the sixth century BCE (when Buddha was born) through the seventh century CE (the time of Harṣavardhana, a king renowned for his Buddhistic conviction and practice), Indian society – passing as it was through several major dynastic changes and shifting patterns of trade and economic activities – stood exposed to a continuous tension persisting between the forces of Hindu revivalism (primarily of the Śaiva tradition) and those of the Buddhist schools of thought and the religious preaching of the Buddhists. If we focus on socially available representations, keeping issues of love and friendship in mind, classical Sanskrit drama, depicting parts of the *Rāmāyaṇa* and the *Mahābhārata* in new forms, developed side by side with the elaborate portrayal of secular urban life by playwrights whose true identity and exact dates have not been ascertained in every case by social and literary historians. Stories of courtly love came to the fore during this period. The *Kathāsaritsāgara* – which strikes readers of our times as comparable to the tales of Sindbad the sailor from the *Arabian Nights* – provided another source of love-stories, drawing attention to the Indian sailors and merchants leaving home for the open sea and foreign lands.

In the context of our project, stories of love and of friendship, of course, are only half the story. Whatever conceptualizations we may choose to read into narratives from early India, they cannot be seriously attributed to their authors. For conceptual characterizations that belong to that period, we must turn to Vātsyāyana's classic articulation of the principles of the art of loving. His *Kāmasūtra*, composed between the third and the fourth century CE, earned Vātsyāyana a place of eminence in the world of Indian philosophy as a thoughtful spokesman of heterodox standpoints. It has been argued that Vātsyāyana's enterprise of combining the *brahmacarya-dharma* and the *nāgarika-vr̥tti* – the way of abstinence and the life of urbanity – sought to establish a systematic association between higher (spiritual) phenomena and lower (bodily) needs.

Vātsyāyana's *Kāmasūtra* was a comprehensive, three-volume treatise. Later works such as Koka-Paṇḍita's *Ratirahasya* (The Mysteries of Loving) and Kalyāṇa-Malla's *Anaṅga-Raṅga* (The Pleasures of the Erotic) were more concise; these accessible works were intended for ordinary readers interested in knowing more about the art of love. That these shorter works, drawing on the source-material available in the *Kāmasūtra*, appeared between the eleventh and the fourteenth centuries suggests that teaching men how to win the hearts of women struck Indians in the south and the north alike as a worthwhile enterprise – for appropriate male pedagogues to take up and systematize.

The serious systematization by Vātsyāyana referred to the traditional hierarchy of *puruṣārthas*, cardinal aims of life, and characteristically chose to subordinate *kāma* (pleasure, eros) to *dharma* (righteousness) and *artha* (material interests), in keeping with the stand that major orthodox thinkers had taken. What places him on the heterodox side of the divide is his individualism: he proposed that each individual, on the basis of his predispositions, his social status, his age, should consciously arrive at a decision as to the prime object in his life.

These moves were being made in a context that is not easy for contemporary Indians to imagine. Thomas observes that intellectual discussion about the status and nature of *kāma* took place in an uninhibited and objective atmosphere in ancient India.

> Ancient Hindu writers had been in a peculiarly favorable position to study erotics. Polygyny was permissible and kings, nobles and wealthy merchants had a plurality of wives and well-stocked harems. A study of sex was not considered indecent or irreligious, and the mediaeval society was ruled by courtesans who were considered adornments of a city.[16]

The Jātaka stories collected and narrated in the Buddhist tradition over several centuries (from apparently the fourth century CE onwards) also speak of courtesans being transformed into devout disciples within the Buddhist order. These facts provide the social context for the claim by Humphreys that, in the culture of Buddhism, the freedom of women is taken seriously. Indeed, if a woman changes completely when she becomes a monk, she can be free and blissful in the sense in which any monk can attain freedom and bliss. Does anything remain of her femininity in the process, however? If there is no femininity left after the transformation, it is disingenuous to claim that she is a "free woman": at best, one could describe her as a free individual devoid of gender identity. And yet we notice that she is a nun, a *bhikkhuṇī* (and not a monk, a *bhikkhu*) – who by virtue of her gender is subordinated to all *bhikkhu*s within the Sangha. Even as a monk, a woman continues to be identified linguistically as well as in other forms of social interaction as a woman, even though she has been made to surrender all her distinctions of femininity.

---

[16] P. Thomas, *Kama Kalpa; or, the Hindu Ritual of Love*, Bombay: D.B. Taraporevala, 1960, p. 76.

This dilemma associated with the gender dichotomy was configured somewhat differently in the Hindu context, which Thomas describes in the following terms without going into the "women's question":

> The author of *Ananga-Ranga* observed that in this world of passing shadows there was but one reality, and that was the pleasure of the company of women. It was equal, he wrote, if not superior to the pleasure of union with Infinite, the Bliss of the ascetic and the mystic.[17]

Indeed, Kalyāṇa-Malla appears to have been willing to go beyond Vātsyāyana and recognize *kāma* as the highest of the *puruṣārtha*s, the aims of life; however, pursuing this issue does not help us to get a clear sense of the texture of the discussion of the erotic in ancient India.

In virtually any serious discussion of *kāma* in the Indian context, it is Śiva who comes into prominence, rather than the figure of Kr̥ṣṇa from Rādhā and Kr̥ṣṇa's captivating love-story. Śiva was married to Pārvatī, and theirs was an exemplar of conjugal love. Forms of marriage mentioned in the scriptures also become salient in the discussion. Indian theory and practice accorded high priority to sacramental marriage, for a man without a wife is not technically qualified to perform his *dharma* as a householder. A virtuous wife, wedded to him with all the appropriate rites, makes the householder's life complete. Tempering this insistence on virtue with realism, however, the social code addressed emergencies arising out of short-lived and ill-directed passion by recognizing as valid "marriages" even those liaisons where the families had not been consulted or other departures from the norm had occurred.

The marriage of Śiva and Pārvatī is a theme we come across not only in the Purāṇa stories, but also in classical Sanskrit

---

[17] Thomas, op. cit.

dramas and folk representations. The tradition of writing long poems in Bengali focused on a particular deity in order to make the hagiography surrounding that deity vivid to the general public – such poems were known as Maṅgala-Kāvyas – gave pride of place to compositions about the household of Śiva and Pārvatī projecting aspects of the Bengali ethos on to those divine figures. There is an element of irony in these writings that portray Lord Śiva the ascetic as a poor and disorganized householder desperately trying to win his lady's favour.

Thomas noted this and other incongruities in the mythology of Śiva available in popular writings and came to the conclusion that Śiva, represented by the phallic *liṅgam*, could not be related to the Vedic tradition, even though the devotees of Śiva took considerable pains to establish the position (which they still maintain) that Śiva is identical with the Vedic god Rudra. We need not worry about unsettled issues in the history of religious ideas as such; however, to the extent that myths affect and shape the social psyche, we do have to examine myths and their implications with some care. The various representations of Śiva, and the myths associated with this iconography, offer a rich field of investigation for social theorists. Focusing on one aspect of this intriguing array of facts, Thomas observes, with some surprise, that

> Shiva, the god of virility, is an enemy of Kāma, the god of sensuality.[18]

Wendy O'Flaherty, in her penetrating study, refers to the "central paradox of Śaiva mythology" which consists in casting the same Śiva figure as both ascetic and erotic. She observes:

> The myths make the Hindu aware of the struggle and of its futility. They show him that his society demands of him

[18] Thomas, op. cit.

> two roles which he cannot possibly satisfy fully – that he beget sons, and that he renounce life and seek union with god. (. . .) The myth makes it possible to admit that the ideal is not attainable.[19]

The way Wendy O'Flaherty construes *bhakti* in the context of the responses of the devotees is helpful when we take a closer look at her approach to these issues. *Bhakti* is for her "one irrational answer to the insoluble problem (. . .)".[20] She sees Śiva's wife Pārvatī as a figure appreciating the fact that her ascetic Lord pities his devotees. In O'Flaherty's view, it is through this move in the myth that "the austere logical purity of Śiva" was transcended and "a merciful sentimentality" introduced.

In the context of our approach, this or any other variant of "merciful sentimentality" would of course serve ends that are quite remote from "the compassion" of the Buddha. And yet, historically, *bhakti* has proved capable of making the figures of Śiva and Buddha converge. One finds instances of Śiva and Buddha merged into one at certain points of the historical development of "the harmonized unity of the Indo-Javanese civilization". It has been remarked that

> the Brahmanism of the Javanese courts was throughout predominantly though not exclusively Saiva. No traces remain of any early Hinayana Buddhism in Java. The Mahayana as a separate and integral cult belongs mainly to the period of Sumatran rule in Central Java; even at this time it is of a Tantrik character, later it becomes increasingly so, and as in Nepal, in Cambodia, and in Bali at the present day, Buddhism and Saiva Hinduism are inseparably combined: Kertanagar received the posthumous name of Sivabuddha".[21]

---

19 Wendy Doniger O'Flaherty, 1973, *Siva: The Erotic Ascetic*, London: Oxford University Press, paperback edn. 1981, p. 38.

20 O'Flaherty, ibid.

21 Ananda K. Coomaraswamy, 1927, *History of Indian and Indonesian Art*, New York: Dover, p. 201.

The conception of the active principle in the universe as feminine which characterizes Indian thinking acquires thematic relevance in the Śiva-Śakti legends (with the Śakti principle concretized in the figure of Pārvatī). The Sāṁkhya system's duality of *puruṣa* and *prakṛti* provides a philosophical frame for the development of this notion. The notion of the *prapañca* – which can be rendered as the "stage", in the sense of the podium on which all performances and processes play out, a notion referred to earlier – can be usefully equated with the metaphysical notion of *prakṛti* (nature), the activizing Śakti (energy or power). In Indian legends and religious discourse, every god's Śakti is visualized as his consort. Among the three principal godheads Brahmā, Viṣṇu and Maheśvara (Śiva), who represent the forces of creation, order and destruction, the force that is responsible for balancing all the forces is Viṣṇu. One way to visualize Śakti is to declare that in principle Śakti is intrinsically Vaiṣṇavī Śakti, associated with the balancing godhead Viṣṇu. At the moment of the dissolution of the cosmos, Śakti activizes Śiva, leading him to dance his cosmos-dissolving *pralaya*-dance and disintegrate the harmonious whole, so that energy is released for new creation. In principle, Śakti manifested as the distinct but related powers of creation (of balanced order and of disorderly destruction) is identical to Śakti in the form of loving joy and vibrant youth manifested as Rādhā, the consort of Viṣṇu's incarnation Kṛṣṇa. On this view, Śakti in all its manifestations is one and the same power, belonging to Viṣṇu who is the force preserving the game of life through all its stages, in both senses of the term "stage".[22]

Such a declaration of the intrinsically Viṣṇu-laden nature of Śakti is not a formulation acceptable to all Hindus. Not all Hindus are Śāktas. Hindus can choose to sing the praises of Śakti as Viṣṇu-Śakti, giving primacy to Viṣṇu, or to adhere to

---

22 Sasibhusan Das Gupta, *Sri Rādhār Kromobikash*, Calcutta: A. Mukherjee & Co., 3rd edn. 1370 BE [CE 1963].

the doctrine that it is Siva's activity or dance-rhythm that is to be equated with Śakti.

> The Shaktas maintain that Shakti pervades all, that the whole universe is her emanation, that she is without form or qualities, vast and imperceptible, the creator, preserver and destroyer of the universe all in one. But it is difficult to worship Shakti in the abstract, and for the benefit of the spiritually dull she is endowed with forms.[23]

It is well known that Tantra, with its emphasis on the feminine principle of active power, became a dominant force in late Buddhism. This development need not surprise us if we remember Buddha's emphasis on "causality" at the expense of "substance". There is no metaphysical incongruity that prevents us from imagining a possible history in which such a world-view, even during Buddha's lifetime, merges into the Indian mainstream for which "Śakti" was ubiquitous and of prime importance. That such a confluence did not happen, I would like to speculate, was primarily because of Buddha's presence, which exuded a *friendly compassion* dissociated from all variants of the notion of *power*.

---

[23] Thomas, op. cit., p. 119.

3

The Contemporary Indian Scene

Constructs and Response Patterns

EVERY society is nurtured by ideologies and cultural constructs which are restructured from time to time by conscious effort. The social climate, saturated with literary-philosophical ideas and discourse, affects the psyche of the people in all societies, but it is difficult to bring this impact to the surface of one's consciousness. Ordinary people, at the level of their daily work and conversation, take it that what they are doing is to draw from immediate experience, from the currently accepted code of conduct, and to take at face value what look to them like successes and failures; in accepting these descriptions, ordinary people do not find it appropriate to connect the prevalent societal mores with basic tenets of classical texts and scriptures that underlie the judgements of actions and their consequences in terms of success and failure.

Similarly, the way oral traditions shape contemporary perceptions and attitudes does not become a matter of conscious reflection for most persons. It is normal to adhere, spontaneously, to customary modes of speech and action, unless something *makes* it necessary to reflect on one's own actions, or the actions of others. At work or in the company of one's friends, one does not ordinarily get into a reflective frame of mind.

Religious congregations in India, however, provide a context in which questions that are not ordinarily raised in the course of one's daily life do become objects of reflection. Here one faces one's *guru*, or one's *bābā*, and seeks access to God who dwells in everybody's heart. The feeling that one should never be evasive here, the tension of being with others engaged in the same quest, makes it possible for people to be more contemplative than they usually allow themselves to be. This changed mood – expressed through a glance, a smile, a bit of whispered monologue or a rapid push forward – are materials eagerly noted by an observer who has come to such a place to study social phenomena associated with love and friendship.

Individual responses observed in a direct face-to-face setting add an element of freshness to a study of society which otherwise would have been a matter of critical analysis of the writings of others coupled with forays into speculative thought. To be sure, the method of direct or naturalistic observation is riddled with problems, which are well known to methodologists and philosophers. And yet, looking at the brief history of methods that rest on observation, it is difficult not to agree with Heynes and Lippitt when they write:

> The informal history of the social observer goes back to the beginning of time. The novelists and the poet have long been concerned with the precise description of social behavior and with deriving propositions about motives and feelings from observed behavior. The average citizen in his day-to-day interactions makes precise observations, especially in areas which are of critical importance to him.[1]

Hoping to be able to bring empirical material concerning love and friendship – primarily from its verbal representations – to bear on the issues explored in this monograph, I entered

[1] Roger U. Heynes and Ronald Lippitt, 1954, "Systematic Observational Technique", in *The Handbook of Social Psychology*, ed. Gardner Lindzey and Elliott Aronson, vol. 1, Reading, Mass.: Addison-Wesley, chapter 10.

group discussions, as a participant-observer, in the setting of religious congregations. I also had occasional opportunities for direct observation of relevant behaviour without disrupting social interaction – the frequency of these opportunities varied across groups and contexts. The use of observer methods in this loose, open-ended manner was in keeping with my goal, which was *not* to *measure* social phenomena in statistical terms on the basis of observation or from secondary sources providing access to quantitative information. The point of this observational supplement to my conceptually and textually anchored study was to obtain relevant spoken and non-verbal material from persons immersed in contemporary Indian culture – material that could be interpreted as defining or manifesting the content of words for "love" and "friendship" in this culture today. The purpose was to corroborate the literary evidence considered in the rest of this monograph by obtaining data – verbal articulations and interactions – through the observation of individuals-in-groups.

The groups that framed such discussion were very small; they comprised two to four persons. One exception needs to be noted – a medium-sized group composed of postgraduate students and research scholars. I also conducted exclusive, open-ended interviews, some within religious congregations, some outside this setting. The average age of the participants was 34.5. The oldest individual under observation was 64 and the youngest, 19. Four large groups covered in this study were audience groups – not engaged in conversation or discussion. Apart from these, seven sittings of medium-sized groups were observed in session with the nodal person (whom one may call the "chief" of the "centre"), singing *bhajana*s and speaking to each other.

Let me place the materials collected through my observations, for expository convenience, in the reverse order – beginning with the seven sittings just mentioned.

Religious gatherings have a fixed place and a more or less firm schedule of activities in most places in India. But Sagar, with "S" as the chief, is different. Evening gatherings are held on a sprawling verandah. The participants come in two at a time, or in slightly larger groups, take off their shoes, and sit there, waiting for *her* to come and join them. "S" has a seat of her own, slightly elevated. She comes, sits down and joins the conversation, sparingly (she never delivers discourses); when somebody says something, she listens, with a pleasant smile. Her apparel is white; she does not change for the evening gathering, even though (here I am reporting what I know through continuous observation) she has had the same dress on while engaged in the chores of the kitchen along with the residents of the ashram after her early morning bath. "S" keeps her long hair loose, but never casually touches it, nor does she ever rearrange her hair. The *bindī* on her forehead is not smudged, for she does not perspire. The residents, mostly women, talk loudly, they call her by her first name, and in their movements they indicate their sense of a special claim over "S" not available to the rest of the group assembled on the verandah. When singing begins, no one sings along. "S" occasionally asks for some songs from others; volunteers then take over for a short while. No pre-labelled "singers" come to attend the sessions; "S" does not try to locate the musical potential in the group. She herself sings in a trained, melodious voice. The singing is followed by a ritualistic prayer to the deity and distribution of oblation by the old man, who is one of two male members of the inner circle of the residents. Dinner follows; but in the meantime everyone will have moved into the hall, which has images and photographs arranged in a corner decorated as a replica of a temple. The group does not look at the corner; their eyes remain riveted on the television set; the evening programme is on. "S" sits with them and watches television for a while. On Sundays the television programme precedes the singing session; in the middle of the television show, "S" gets up and gently moves to the verandah. The group follows her very gradually, one by one. It is difficult to predict who will come out first to sit near "S" or in front of her. The group settles down, and then disperses again to watch the rest of the show. If some significant part of the programme is missed, the residents whisper to each other half-jokingly about the loss. Dinner is served by the residents; they take turns. "S" has a separate bowl and dishes; she eats her food on a small table; the others sit, facing her, on floor mats, in a row or in several rows, depending on the number of diners. Lunch is served very early because there is no breakfast; very few outsiders join the lunch, apart from special occasions. "S" starts her meal with everybody else, but stays at her table much longer because she chats while she eats. Others, busily chewing, silently listen, smiling every once in a while, or bursting into laughter. "S"'s humorous conversation seems to please them. She retires to her room around 9.30 (the time is not rigidly fixed) and spends her time there in peace and quiet. However, the doors to her room remain open – only the curtains are drawn – and women in adjoining rooms chat among themselves for some more time. The presence of an observer with no command over Telugu is accepted without comment. That "S" attracts English-speaking people is known to all.

How does this place so near the roaring sea and so distant from the changing cities in India differ from similar households at Bheemunipatnam, or any other seaside village in India? Does a householder in the adjoining locality run the household in such a way that Sagar stands out as an ashram? I observed the daily life of some householders (as much as I could, with my limited resources) to find an answer. One typical household that was observed is run along the following lines. The householder is well-to-do, gentle and hospitable. The house, carefully built and richly decorated, is pleasant to look at. It carries a nameplate near the gate. Visitors are received by the maid, who is very courteous. She has been properly trained in the art of housekeeping by the lady of the household. She has also learnt middle-class etiquette; the householders are able to introduce her to visitors and guests as "our daughter". TV programmes, newspapers and magazines, gardening, occasional visits and playing cards over the weekend keep this retired householder engaged. Their children are all grown up and settled abroad with their own well-planned families. They visit their children occasionally; the lady stays on, as she knows that, back home, their housekeeper (daughter-in-residence) will keep the house and the head of the family in perfect shape while her NRI children enjoy their mother's company a little bit longer. The family photographs of these happy visits are carefully preserved and shared with friends and visitors. Food is cooked and served by their "daughter"-housekeeper. This is just a random example; is it suggestive?

At Sagar, the labour of preparing food is shared (as has already been described). There is no maid. "S" is the acknowledged "head" of the Sagar household. But all residents of this ashram – an ashram that is analogous to a household at one level – know that "S" is *not* their provider; financial support for Sagar residents is provided by well-to-do householders (including landholders and small but thriving business-houses). Daughter, mother and other kinship terms are not in use here. What draws these people to Sagar is not something which could be ascertained by observation alone. There were conversations, between the observer and those members of the group (residents included) who had some English. "S" sat with the observer during three sessions.

Data collected from Prashanti-Nilayam at Puttaparthi present a very different set-up; interactions there take place under the "direction" of "Bābā", whose presence is felt all over the area even when he is not in view. "Bābā" truly stands as a father to his devotees. At the time of the observation reported here, in 1986, "Bābā" was not "materializing" gems or any other precious objects; we found him right in the middle of his new educational project and no longer in the mood to show "miracles"; but his personal appearance every morning and every afternoon worked as a miracle. The large audience would wait in silence, intently expecting something to happen any moment.

People from places near and far bring clothes and other objects to receive "Bābā"'s touch; presents are also given, which "Bābā" himself does not take; the volunteers, under the guidance of senior devotees in charge of various units, handle those matters – speaking in whispers to each other. "Bābā" moves through the encircled area with measured steps, once in a while stopping by someone and permitting that devotee – that child, or woman, or man – to touch his feet, sometimes scribbling *oṁ* on the slate held up by the devotee, with a smile or a quiet side-glance. When he suddenly changes his course and walks back or walks away from a particular row, a gasp is heard at once from the audience. Every move, every step by "Bābā" is watched by everyone in the assembly with painful alertness. He is in view for about twelve minutes – or for fifteen minutes on special occasions, such as giving away new garments to school-children. These garments, prepared under "Bābā"'s instructions, are handed to him by a devotee who holds a formal position at the ashram. "Bābā", clad in his usual saffron, looks at the basket, smiles, and begins to give these colourful clothes to a group of youngsters, specifically assembled for the purpose, one by one, each greeting him brightly. A Swedish lady in the audience (a resident at Prashanti-Nilayam for more than a decade) is moved to tears; "there is no limit to Bābā's compassion", she whispers to herself. She has picked up enough Telugu to offer help to those who want to get seated near the route "Bābā" is likely to take when he walks through the assembly to make his appearance.

"Bābā"'s open air appearance and his return to the covered area of the temple take place at fixed hours; the *bhajana* singing and the oblation also follow a strict schedule. Devotees and visitors have to queue up for food in the common kitchen at fixed times. Everything is done in an orderly fashion and, as far as possible, without visible tension. Roving devotees, chanting and singing *bhajanas*, announce the break of the day. Most of the visitors/guests residing within the area of Prashanti-Nilayam join in, but there is no compulsion about joining in this morning round.

Every morning and evening, the daily prayers, *bhajana*-singing and the *darśana* (an audience with "Bābā") are attended by everyone. The largest gathering within the period under study, on Guru-Pūrṇimā day in 1986, attracted pilgrims from various places. There was a lady from Singapore who had no accommodation; she accepted a great deal of hardship only to have a close view of "Bābā" (and perhaps his blessings as well). Disappointed, she turned bitter. "Even a god should know how to behave himself", she murmured. Addressing the public within the covered area, "Bābā" keeps the entire assembly (both inside the auditorium and outside where they can hear but not see him) mesmerized with his talk and singing. The songs he sings are set to well-known folk tunes; the lyrics are his own; a large part of the audience joins in. His discourse in Telugu is interpreted into English over the microphone – the interpretation is consecutive, but the work is done so smoothly that one hardly notices that technically it is not simultaneous interpretation. When "Bābā" finds the rendering inaccurate, he interrupts his talk and corrects the interpreter.

The set-up, programme and daily routine are so differently

structured from the common households in India that the identity of Prashanti-Nilayam as an ashram stands out. The entire place is an ongoing project, with its workshops, discourse, educational programmes and social work. Certain devotees become office bearers, with responsibilities formally assigned for specified periods. They interact with each other as members of a large, extended family-group. Kinship terms are used in this group among the devotees, "Bābā" (father) providing the stable frame of reference. Cottages belonging to the families of some devotees within the ashram boundary do indeed belong to "Bābā"; Sai Samity (the association of Sathya-Saibaba) keeps the keys, and determines who shall be entitled to use the living quarters when these families are absent. "Bābā" does not permit any individual devotee or any family to stay for any length of time away from their work in other places. Thus, everybody staying at Puṭṭaparthi is a transitory visitor, except for those devotees who are engaged in prolonged assignments of teaching, or giving medical treatment to the patients and caring for the disabled at the hospital. For ordinary devotees, visiting Prashanti-Nilayam is like coming home on vacation. "Bābā" refreshes them not by any special effort, but just by being what he is, a father caring for all. A devotee who happened to be a "very good organizer" working for the community's Sevā Dal, its volunteer group which mobilizes the young for social work, dies in Calcutta. Devotees from the Calcutta chapter mourn this loss in whispers with tears in their eyes. "Last time 'Bābā' said everything would be all right", someone whispers, without complaining. Someone else responds, "Yes, he meant to say that she would be in peace – and she is. There is no cure for cancer yet. Bābā sent sacred ashes to her; she did feel good when she touched the ashes; and you see, the attending doctor writes how blissfully she passed away, without pain or regret". The devotees do believe that "Bābā" is a miracle-worker, a god in this slender mortal frame, and yet, when no miraculous cure is possible, they trust "Bābā" if he *chooses* not to permit a miracle in a particular case. He who can intervene in the natural state of affairs can also choose *not* to intervene.

In the very different community at Sagar, apparently similar thinking underlies the faith of the residents in special powers that "S" is believed to have, although she has never demonstrated any. In fact, "S"'s critics describe as a failure on her part her actions in the year of the Aṣṭa-graha-sammelana, the alignment of eight planets. She predicted a deluge. Her father, then residing at Tiruvannamalai, who believed in her new spiritual power (he believed that she had undergone a psychic transformation and that the god spoke through her), wrote to innumerable people throughout south India and urged them to take refuge near "S" to survive the catastrophe. Crowds came; nothing happened; "S" told the baffled crowd that she had decided to hold back the deluge; that too was within her power. Some of the residents told me this story over and over again, without the slightest trace of disbelief in their voice, although they were aware that I had heard another version of the events from skeptics.

Many of these devotees have been with "S" since the time of her youth in Tiruvannamalai, when she was a girl of considerable beauty, fond of fashionable attire and Western perfumes, all of which she has given up since. Her father, the devotees say, had a heart of gold; common standards of morality cannot measure him. A creative writer by inspiration and a teacher by profession in Andhra, her father Chalam exerted great influence not only on his first-born daughter "S", but also on nearly two generations of youth in southern India through his writing. Born in 1894 and exposed to the nineteenth-century Brahmo movement in his youth, Chalam met Rabindranath Tagore when the latter was in transit at Vijayawada; he translated *Gitanjali* into Telugu. He was initiated into Brahmoism, but did not remain a Brahmo. He lost faith and became an agnostic. His second major redirection of energies began with his first visit to Tiruvannamalai, the dwelling-place of Bhagavān Ramaṇa Maharṣi, in 1936. "S" accompanied her father on one of his early visits to the Bhagavān's ashram in 1938. When Chalam eventually moved his household – a household marked by his extraordinary policy of keeping his door open to women in distress – to Tiruvannamalai, in 1950, for him this decision to resettle there was a matter of bringing closure to decades of being torn between irreconcilable goals in his life. If it was his intention to spend some years in physical proximity to the Bhagavān, that, however, was not to be; just a few months after he and "S" had completed their shift of residence, Ramaṇa Maharṣi passed away.

For "S", the shift of residence and new living arrangements for the household represented the unfolding of a "divine plan". Well after Bhagavān Ramaṇa Maharṣi's terrestrial passing, the Bhagavān – the "Īśvara" – spoke to "S" in a dream and made her "realize" that she was "both masculine and feminine". Her conversion did not come about through any ritualistic initiation – there appear not to have been any ritual elements in the dream. Even after this conversion, she did not renounce her family bonds: her allegiance to her father (who died in 1979) remained undisturbed; this stands in contrast to other seekers – including Ramaṇa Maharṣi himself – whose transformation involved leaving their family, physically and spiritually.

The ashram that "S" runs is called "Sagar" to recall her association with the Bhagavān. It is one of several centres that function in and around Andhra in the name of Bhagavān Ramaṇa Maharṣi. These very different units keep in touch, exchange information and take help from one another as and when this is compatible with the scheme of social work that has evolved at each place. Their schemes are not formally articulated programmes in any sense of the term; what they have in common is an awareness and respect for individual freedom – a value propagated by Ramaṇa Maharṣi. "S" in her exclusive interview for the present study says,

> This is what my two gurus had in common. They had otherwise very different dispositions. My father was a real artist, combining the fine, feminine qualities with masculine vigour and uprightness. This is what I am too.

She would not venture to explicitly describe the character traits of Ramaṇa Maharṣi, the sublime, cheerful ascetic who drew her out of the petty privacy of her early adolescence, not by outward pressure or persuasion but inwardly arousing in her "the most intense, all-consuming love" she had ever experienced. She was so full of it at the time of her "critical moment" that there was no room for personal intimacy: He *was* she herself, the two blended in one – "S" does not invoke the idea of "Ardhanārīśvara", of Śiva blending into Pārvatī; on the contrary, she says, "I am Śiva". That was the moment of her ecstasy and of great suffering as well, for she had to come to terms with her changed self. She changed her way of life. She remembers how her father helped her by perfect non-interference. In fact, he became a devotee of hers, according to others who witnessed the transformation "S" went through and the change in her relationship with her father. After her father's death, "S" and the other residents left Tiruvannamalai. She likes this place by the sea with a hill nearby. Moving to a city is not an option she even considers. She wishes to stay in a quiet place and fulfil her mission. She has a sense of mission, but does not want to speak about it to people "in search of a message" from her; "they are to find it freely, on their own. Discourse is a compulsion. No compulsion can ever be a help in one's search for truth". She believes in *love*, *peace* and *silence*.

"S" differentiates friendship from love in terms of intensity and immediacy:

> Love burns you up from within, whereas friendship soothes you with words, work, jokes, all from outside. Friendship offers sustenance to you – whoever you are. Love challenges you to change.

"S" values the saying *A friend in need is a friend indeed,* and its Indian counterpart referred to earlier.

A close friend of hers, "R" – who does not live in the ashram, but in another town – did not dwell much on the purifying aspect of love ("burning is purification") when interviewed. As she sees it, "Love is a fulfilment without which there can be no real 'peace'." Is friendship also a form of 'love' that brings the friends fulfilment? "R" is not sure.

Members of the outer circle of the elite in the small locality responded to the question of "love" more or less along the same lines as "R". Among them, "N" elaborated his idea of friendship; from the discussion with him it emerged that on his view "true friends" serve as what sociologists have called "reference groups". One attaches great importance to the approval and admiration of these people (one's "true friends"). "N" also observes that "true friendship runs through life, even if frequent meetings are not possible".

The idea of love that emerges in conversations at Prashanti-Nilayam is something marked by the spirit of self-sacrifice. "You do things for the person you love." The mother's love for her child serves as the paradigm. Everyone there also agrees that without love there can be no peace, but they add that the proof of love lies in the dedication that you bring to your work; that is what "Bābā" says. A mentally ill girl keeps coming back to Prashanti-Nilayam, and refuses to go back. Devotees are upset. "Bābā" wants her to be removed and taken back to "her people" in her hometown. Love as "work" cannot permit irregularities. Prashanti-Nilayam has efficient organizers; moving a girl (who was suffering from deep schizophrenic delusions) away from the area without force involved devising an appropriate method; this was done without much difficulty.

In his discourses (in summer groups and on special occasions), (Sri) Sathya Sai Bābā draws from scriptures and epics, combining these references with fables and tales as well as stories taken from real life. He speaks on the basis of received notions of morality, adding flavour through innovative variations. His speeches are published in English in the volumes of *Sathya Sai Speaks*, which have been appearing regularly. "Bạbā" sees his mission very clearly (and makes it known to others through his programme and preaching); the mission is to revive the old values, which are eternal, and to improve the conditions in which people live. As a non-brāhmaṇa god-man, (Sri) Sathya Sai could conceivably have been taken to be a reincarnation of Kr̥ṣṇa; however, in his case as well, people see Śiva revealed through him. Devotees take the well-known *Daśāvatāra-Stotra* as their basis when they sing *Jaya Jagadīśa Hare*, with variations, at the end of their *bhajana* sessions; they show no interest in the riddle of the Śiva–Viṣṇu duality. Basic conceptual questions are not raised; but discussions do take place on matters of definition and classification as they emerge from a discourse.

Sai Bābā honours the custom of keeping men and women in separate areas in the audience; they come into the enclosure through separate entrances, which are far from each other. He is not accessible for exclusive interviews; he never has been, the devotees say. His life-story is that of a god-man available to regular devotees and to visitors who want an audience. The narratives of his formative years are full of miracles. All this makes Prashanti-Nilayam as strikingly different from Sagar as two ashrams could possibly be. Sai

Bābā is indeed very different from "S", although they both speak Telugu.

The group discussions for the present study were held in a relaxed but academic atmosphere. They were based on questions, counter-questions with no pressure to come to a solution of the issues raised. Senior students, research scholars and teachers were involved in these conversations. A small number of (educated) housewives were also available for discussion. Younger people (students, teachers) resisted the attempt by others to encourage them to open up and give their views on "love". Talking about "friendship" was easier, especially because many of them meant "acquaintance" when they used the word "friend". Once this confusion was recognized, there arose a difficulty: how could "true" friendship be differentiated from "love"? At this point in the conversation, it became possible to bring "love" too into the discussion, by way of comparisons with friendship. Literature and films provide models for "love"; participants were able to use these models freely when they needed to make a point. "Why is it that we don't have stories or films about 'friends'?" – some of them asked.

A majority of the participants mentioned "intensity" as the characteristic mark of "love" and added that, of course, "love" has a social aim, marriage. Love is considered to be "successful" when it ends in a happy marriage. Failure in love can take two forms: if the couple in love do not get married; or if, in the course of their married life, their pre-marital warmth is lost. The question of "success" and "failure" does not apply to the context of friendship. One may lose track of friends, or they may die, but such events do not count as failures of the friendship itself. A friend who turns against a friend becomes a "treacherous person", whom one can no longer regard as a "friend". What about a friend who shows "intense" emotion and turns into a lover, or tries to? The fact that such situations do arise in real life prompted the participants to consider "intensity" as a major differential separating "love" from "friendship".

Another differential identified by many participants had to do with the "private/public" distinction. A certain ambiguity in the use of the word "private" was evident here; several participants made the point that, whereas "love" requires privacy in the sense of exclusiveness, one can hardly confide in one's lover/beloved. Only a friend can be a confidant, invoking a sense of privacy that is not available in the context of love. This inevitably leads to complications by admitting the need for the actual or imagined presence of a third person – playing the role of a friend or confidant – affecting the private life of the couple, intruding into their "privacy". There is another type of complication that can arise: the confidant may turn into a trespasser in the psychic area reserved for lovers alone, making one of the partners jealous. This topic led to the discovery of yet another differential – the fact that love and friendship are very differently situated on the "tension vs. relaxation" dimension. "Love" is a state of tension, requiring constant attentiveness and aiming for release; in comparison, "friendship" is much more relaxed and – as "S" says in her comments – "soothing".

Some participants suggested that in true, mature love, the couple attains deep mutual understanding and confidence in each other. Whether it makes sense to distinguish between the maturity of the love itself and the maturity of the persons who are in love was a controversial question. Some participants admitted that a "new" love (no matter how "mature" the person falling in love might be) is always vulnerable, open to jealousy and tension. This admission takes away the hallmark of "love" – its single-minded faithfulness. How could one have more than one "new" love in one's life if true love is unique?

Steadfast loyalty remains a crucial issue in group

discussions held on this topic in Andhra and in West Bengal. *Enki-Patalu* – songs of Enki, in rural varieties of Telugu – depict lovers whispering to each other of their togetherness in previous births and destined to last for many more births, including of course their present intimacy, thus affirming their deep faith in the steadfastness of love, which uniquely defies mortality. This enduring character of true love is celebrated by the permanent tie of sacramental marriage; so at least it seemed to the participants in group discussions in West Bengal. In the groups in Andhra, the discussion revolved around questions of how love flourishes differently in the climate of individual freedom – citing the evergreen story of Rādhā and Kṛṣṇa's love as well as some writings by "S"'s father Chalam; the point that emerged was that true love, though its experience projects a sense of constancy, does not in and of itself require formalization in terms of eternal marital bonding. That true love must lead to a blissful marriage is a romantic idea which does not appear to correspond to authentic Indian conceptions of love, judging by what is shown in the epics and other writings from early India. Rabindranath Tagore, in his depiction of love, remained true to the Indian tradition.

Bedtime stories told by Indian grandmothers offer a wonderful world where faultless young princes end up winning the hearts of exquisitely beautiful princesses (and their hand in marriage), often with the help of small animals and birds, after defeating several kinds of demons and fierce, large animals in direct combat – excellent material for wish-fulfilling dreams. In these children's stories, marriage does count as celebrating a person's achievement and as providing ultimate security and love. Even though the comparison is not often made (because our discussions of the cinema tend to trace all phenomena in films to Western origins), the fact remains that average "boy-meets-girl" stories from the studios of Bombay, Chennai and Calcutta [*editorial note: this monograph was written in 1988 – in that period Chennai had already been renamed, but Mumbai and Kolkata had not*] offer a modern variant of the bedtime stories our grandmothers used to tell. It was Rabindranath Tagore who emphatically noted the value and validity of these tales as stimuli for a young child's mental development. When he heard those stories as a growing child – he writes – he said to himself: "That good, brave prince is none but I". There is no call to accept this as a solid fact to be added to a biography of Tagore; but it does tell us a great deal about Tagore's concept of nurture – and of love.

Tagore's depictions of love among adults and his joyful descriptions of the child's yearning for the mother's undivided attention and admiration situate "love" at two different levels of vivid passion. How these modes of passion tie up with the all-encompassing human love of beauty, which is another dimension of the human quest for balanced and valid formulations of the truth, is a question he explores throughout his long, creative life as a visionary poet, a social thinker, a worker in the field of music, drama and painting. His playful uses of incongruity and absurdity in the fantasy genre writings for children that he produced in the last decade of his life (such as *Sey*, an intriguing text whose title is a pronoun that refers not to someone you can see "here" or "there" in the visual field, but to someone absent – thus verging on a pronoun for "the Other") stand in need of a serious, in-depth study yet to be attempted. Given the unavailability of such analyses, I can only refer to his earlier poems for children, many of which are written in the first person (such as the well-known *Birpurush*, "the hero"[2]) to illustrate the idea elaborated in the following prose passage where Tagore links his ideal of education with his understanding of the place of love in

---

[2] [***Editor's note***: For an English rendering, see "The Hero", in William Radice (tr.), 1985, *Rabindranath Tagore: Selected Poems*, Harmondsworth: Penguin, pp. 68-69.]

children's lives. Tagore writes:

> Children are living beings – more living than the grown-up people who have built shells of habit around themselves. Therefore it is absolutely necessary for their mental health and development that they should not have mere schools for their lessons, but a world whose guiding spirit is personal love.[3]

One steady source of this "personal love" is the enthusiastic capacity of women for loving care, says Tagore. In the postscript to a letter to his friend and relative Pramatha Chaudhuri he writes:

> Man is related to this practical world of everyday life primarily through his cognition – not much of a vital tie. The feminine interest in practical matters is truly a vital interest. The way to revive the taste and ardour for life can be found when one receives its touch – can we, only by our reassuring words appealing to his sense of duty [towards life], hope to succeed in bringing a morbid person back to the normal course of life? I doubt (. . .).[4]

This November 1917 letter is not the only one he wrote to Pramatha Chaudhuri on the importance of what is described in today's parlance as "gender" in the area of love and care. In a much earlier letter, in May 1890, Tagore had written:

> (. . .) the yearning for beauty is spiritual, detached from the ties of home, aiming at the formless, whereas love is mundane, tied to the form (. . .). He who loves, gives it to imperfect human beings suffering in deprivation and pain, has to have infinite forgiveness and patience to love – but one who yearns for beauty looks for perfection, and thus his

---

[3] "From *Thoughts from Rabindranath Tagore*", in Amiya Chakravarty (ed.) *A Tagore Reader*, New York: Macmillan, 1961, p. 278. Emphasis mine.

[4] Archival material available in the Pramatha Chaudhuri File, Rabindra Bhavana Collection, Visva-Bharati, Santiniketan.

> desire (for perfection) remains insatiable. Every human being has both of these elements, some imperfection as well as perfection; I think women experience the fullness of perfection in themselves to a greater extent (that is why they can easily be content with any object of love) compared to men, who feel the pinch of their own incompleteness with the result that no amount of knowledge and love keep them perfectly satisfied (. . .).[5]

In his own love for children, however, Tagore appeared to have no "yearning for perfection". The immediate presence of children inspired him immensely, urging him to burst into song to express the joy of fulfilment. In his songs Tagore's spontaneous, personal love for children can be seen as continuous with his love of nature. He easily crosses over from one to the other, as in the passage: "(. . .) When I kiss your face to make you smile, my darling, I surely understand what pleasure streams from the sky in morning light, and what delight the summer breeze brings to my body – when I kiss you to make you smile",[6] or as in the song which begins with nature, *Ei to bhalo legechilo – alor nachon patay patay* "This is what I liked – the dance light from leaf to leaf", and which goes on to describe the beauty of the way children are able to enjoy and participate in the abundant beauty of nature. This song, which brings out particularly well the carefree tone that connects Tagore's nature songs with what he writes about children, is an important point of reference if we are to understand his view.

For him the child is not just a child. Tagore sees the tender, loving form of the child merging into the infinite beauty of nature; he goes further and contends that this is not a matter

---

[5] *Chithipatra* [selected correspondence], vol. 5, Calcutta: Visva-Bharati, 1945, pp. 133-34. Translation mine.

[6] "When and Why", in From *The Crescent Moon*, Chakravarty, op. cit., p. 310.

of his own poetic vision alone, but is rooted in classical India. "According to the true Indian view," Tagore writes, "our consciousness of the world, merely as the sum total of things that exist, and as governed by laws, is imperfect. But it is perfect when our consciousness realises all things as spiritually one with it, and therefore capable of giving us joy" – a joy that Tagore sees particularly clearly manifested in the spontaneity of children, and in the spontaneity an adult regains access to in their company. "For us the highest purpose of this world", Tagore continues, "is not merely living in it, knowing it and making use of it, but realising our own selves in it through expansion of sympathy; not alienating ourselves from it and dominating it, but comprehending and uniting it with ourselves in perfect union."[7]

It may be of interest to note here that in course of the talks delivered in Europe during 1921-22, Tagore even suggested that it was perhaps "(. . .) through the influence of the newly discovered philosophy of India which stirred the soul of Germany and aroused the attention of other Western countries" that Wordsworth and Shelley's attitude towards nature had acquired its specific nuance. There is no room here for a debate over this suggestion; conclusions about the truth or falsity of the claim would hardly change the course of our deliberation. What is of great relevance to us, however, is that Tagore in his conceptualization of love was consciously using a Western frame of reference that he believed to be related to values once cherished in India. The import of his suggestion quoted above is that, although universal love so understood is within everybody's reach in principle, yet it is possible to trace the origin of this response pattern to one particular culture (India in this case) and to investigate how

[7] "The Religion of the Forest", in "From *Creative Unity*", Chakravarty, op. cit., p. 274.

its influence has been diffused to other cultures through direct or indirect contact.

In such an argument, India is given priority. But the Indian tradition seems not to attach much value to priority. The eagerness to look for an original "source" and to relate it to later "developments" in terms of "influence", expecting to be able to bring every single occurrence into well-defined categories governed by a trajectory in terms of a spectrum amenable to theoretical conceptualization, is typically Western. Old religious scriptures, legends and epics as well as folk tales and fables in India speak of events without paying much heed to historical precedence. In these narrations identical themes and ideas are repeated with variations; every version persists, side by side with the others, as discrete units; the overall set of variants has no discernible inner consistency or overall unity, and classical Indian theoreticians have never tried to subsume all these variants under any conceptualization. Tagore brought a different approach to the scene; but he described his enterprise (a proposed unification of what looks like irreconcilable diversity) as a truly Indian approach. His vision of Indian unity is articulated in such passages as this:

> We cannot see clearly the age in which we now live, yet we feel that the India of today has aroused herself once more to find her truth, her harmony, and her oneness, not only among her own people, but with the world. The current of her life, which had been dammed up in stagnation, has found a breach in the wall and can now feel the waves of humanity outside. We shall learn that we can reach the world, not through an effacement, but through an expansion of our own individuality.[8]

Obviously this vision of Tagore's is outspokenly cultural; that he is trying to include "nature" in his vision without any

[8] "A vision of India's History" (1912), Chakravarty, op. cit., p. 194.

residue, however, is equally obvious. In Tagore's vision of history – as well as his idea of religion, which he presented as the poet's religion and which had come to be directly associated with his concept of love – there is a suggestion that culture is an inalienable part of human nature. This suggestion has far-reaching significance; it is appropriate for us only to explore it to the extent that it sheds light on his ideas about women's place in life and love.

To move from love-for-children to love-for-nature and universal love of beauty and innocence appears easy along what is assumed to be a continuum of manifestations of basic trust in "humanity". It appears especially easy if one sets gender differences aside. Children are yet to acquire "gender" – the whole point of the conception of "gender" is to contrast this social construct with nature, where we find sex but not gender. But the surprising fact is that "nature" (*prakṛti*) counts as "feminine" in many human conceptual systems and languages. Tagore was not only familiar with this association of nature with femininity; he was in a sense reaffirming specifically the naturalness of women when he emphasized women's "vital interest" in the everyday world in his letter cited above.

Tagore's vision of harmony and beauty reigning supreme in the universe, including the human order, does not involve nature alone. "Nature" being what it is, particular viewers may find it benign, bountiful, "pleasant-beautiful", harmonious, or on the contrary hostile, "ferocious-attractive", unpredictably open-ended – depending on the mood of the viewer. A romantic wanderer may find both faces of nature "beautiful", as Tagore himself did at certain moments which remain captured in his poems addressed to "Vasundharā" (a word for the earth that portrays it as bountiful) and "Pṛthivī" (another word for the earth, which has become one of its neutral designations in Bengali). There is an undeniable beauty in incongruence and intensity which in practical life might bring great discomfort. Tagore in his writings hailed the ruthless beauty of "nature". Yet when it came to cases of "natural" attraction between men and women, Tagore was unable to take the stance of a permissive spectator. In many of his novels, plays, poems and essays, he is openly critical of lovers seeking union as an aim. His attitude is not to be confused with the ordinary social conservatism and its frankly critical appraisal of love. Tagore values love and the human capacity for love; but in his view the only way to keep true love alive and shining for ever is to keep it free, to remove it from the sphere of the obligations and petty encounters of daily life. In his early writings (e.g. *Mayar Khela* "The Play of *Māyā*", a music-focused opera that he later rewrote in the dance-drama genre) he emphatically distinguishes between the search for youthful pleasure mistaken as love and the acceptance of the value of a person with tenderness and forbearance; he cherished the latter rather than the former in his evaluation of human love. His views stressing the need to distance oneself from passionate love were expressed throughout his creative career; eventually he arrived at a distinction between lower and higher levels in human nature itself. In his play *Lalater Likhan* "Fate", soon rewritten as *Bansari* (1933), where Bansari is a girl in love with the hero, Tagore introduces the character of an ascetic *guru* who, speaking to Bansari, argues that what should form the basis of union between man and woman is *prem* (love as overflowing joy) and not *bhalobasa* (love as personal attachment), for *bhalobasa*, polluted as it is by narrow attachments, is an inferior attraction which all animals have in common; only humans are able to elevate themselves to the level of *prem* – of overflowing, unalloyed joy – to fulfil their mission in life.

Victoria Ocampo, the author who was Tagore's hostess in Argentina in 1924, to whom Tagore reportedly taught only one Bengali word – *bhalobasa* (love) – "remembered Tagore

(. . .) as an artist who had made her understand the meaning of 'Love-Light'".[9] How Ocampo viewed this *Amor-Luz* (Love-Light) in 1927 is described and interpreted by Kushari-Dyson. It is of interest to note that Tagore introduced Ocampo to the inclusive word *bhalobasa* – including what he would later, in *Lalater Likhan*, characterize as *prem*. He was to write of "love-light" himself, in his own way, shortly after his stay in Argentina: "Let my love, like sunlight, surround you/and yet give you illumined freedom".[10] This freedom which illumines as it surrounds is never public; it is felt within, because: "Love remains a secret even when spoken".[11]

Anything loud, obvious and clamouring for possession of another person was condemned by Tagore as an expression of a lower, bestial nature not fit to be considered properly human. In every human heart there is a deep core of privacy which can never be reached if the person trying to reach it is even slightly intrusive or invasive; Tagore believed that love empowered the lover to sense its delicate presence without understanding it all, for no one can fully understand another person. In the context of a personal relationship, the attempt to stretch the limits of human understanding seemed to Tagore to be like trespassing into the inner territory of another person, which belongs to no one other than God. Tagore's "overflowing love", in other words, respects natural boundaries which are inviolable and sacred. This is an ideal he upholds even in the case of the mother–child relation. A mother who nags, or pampers, or dotes on the child does not, in his view, offer true motherly love, but hinders the child's growth. Tagore's reprimand addressed to Mother Bengal for

---

9 Ketaki Kushari-Dyson, 1988, *In Your Blossoming Flower-Garden: Rabindranath Tagore and Victoria Ocampo*, New Delhi: Sahitya Akademi, pp. 225-29.

10 "Fireflies", Chakravarty, op. cit., p. 339.

11 Ibid., p. 340.

making her children mere Bengalis and preventing them from growing up as human beings is a passage all Bengalis are familiar with. In his portrayal of mothers in novels, short stories and sketches, one finds Tagore looking critically at the narrow confines of domestic interest within which mothers in real life moved. His mother-ideal is depicted in the character of Anandamoyee in the novel *Gora*; her overflowing love, like ambrosia, sustains all children in their independent pursuit of righteousness; it is not bestowed on an individual child in response to his or her needs. It is this automatic flow of the mother's love that endows it with supreme value and sanctity.

True love, as Tagore understands it, is about bliss, not pleasure. A love which can endure the test of suffering and is aglow with forgiveness is Tagore's consistent ideal, at all levels of love. The character Kumu in his novel *Jogajog* flags this ideal when she quotes the following passage from the *Bhagavad-Gītā*:

> (. . .) I bow down before Thee and prostrate my body and I demand grace of Thee, the adorable Lord. As a father to his son, as a friend to his friend and comrade, as one dear with him he loves, so should Thou, O Godhead, bear with me".[12]

As has been noted above, love's natural expression in *pleasure* was always suspect in Tagore's world-view. He would compare it with flowers that were beautiful but fated to wilt by the end of the day, leaving men and women to be sustained by the fruits of suffering. This is not to suggest that Tagore sought a way to salvation that involved resolutely avoiding the temptations of perishable pleasures, shutting one's eyes

---

[12] This English translation of the passage from the *Gītā* is quoted from (Sri) Aurobindo's *Essays on the Gita* [(*The Complete Works of Sri Aurobindo*, vol. 19, Pondicherry: Sri Aurobindo Ashram Publication Department, 1997 edn.), p. 389]. Tagore's *Jogajog* renders the Sanskrit passage in Bengali.

to them. On the contrary, he believed in enjoying the majestic diversity of flowers (from a *distance*, letting them be, without creating any disturbance in the natural order of beauty), an enjoyment made poignant by the knowledge that there is no enduring sustenance in them, but a pervading sadness which adds to the glory of transitory forms of beauty. In Tagore's view, only a person with the strength to fearlessly face the sorrow of separation, possibly permanent separation, is entitled to the bliss offered by nature.

A slight variation of this theme is observed when Tagore brings it to bear on the portrayal of conjugal love in his novels. Love of the "overflowing" kind permits freedom in a marital context, a freedom without questions – elevating the relationship to a level at which the new value of mutual trust supersedes the ritualistic prescriptions of orthodoxy regarding the duties of a wife. The Damini–Sribilas couple in the novel *Chaturanga* provides an excellent example. Working on the same model, Nikhilesh in *Ghare-Baire* leads the marriage, and his wife Bimala, to a doom which Tagore, of course, refuses to recognize as a doom: the way he frames the narrative, Bimala is "illumined" by the love of Nikhilesh, which affects her all the more deeply through their suffering. Bimala is as passionate as Damini, and has experienced the tensions of love of the "attachment" type. Immersed from the very beginning of her marriage in the infinite patience and forgiveness of her husband's "overflowing love", Bimala is initially unaware of its value, and is forced to rediscover it – perceiving its reality for the first time – through the severe pain of crisis and disillusionment; whereas Damini, after Shachish arouses passionate love in her, undergoes "death" when he rejects her, and then a catharsis prepares her for a serious, fulfilling marriage with Sribilas, a man who offers her love of the "overflowing" kind. In both of these novels, Tagore depicts relations of friendship between men of unequal abilities. In

Ghare-Baire, he seems to choose to endow Nikhilesh and Sandip with character profiles that are incompatible precisely so that he can illustrate different faces of love.

In *Chokher Bali* – an earlier novel of his that shows the gradual evolution of mature conjugal love, building itself a structure from the debris of earlier phases of pleasurable but frantically passionate episodes of youthful, over-possessive love – friendship serves a different purpose. It is of interest to note that the novel *Chokher Bali* was first rendered into English as *Binodini*; the salient character in the novel is indeed Binodini, whose making friends with Asha marks the beginning of a major disruption in Asha's life. (The title of the novel reflects Binodini and Asha's decision to call each other "Chokher Bali" [eye-sore], using an acknowledged feminine strategy of their social milieu, expressing affection through its opposite.)

Friendship between two girls outside the kinship group is seldom found in Tagore's writings. Binodini in this novel was both a friend and an enemy to Asha – an idea which Tagore did not develop fully. He was writing a family drama in which Mahendra's infatuation, passively encouraged by his mother's doting attachment for her only son, throws his life and his home into disequilibrium – not only when he is madly drawn towards the young widow Binodini, but at the very beginning of the narrative, when, charmed by the youthful innocence of Asha he decides to claim her as his bride, reversing the arrangements that were already in place for Asha to be given in marriage to his close friend Bihari. Mahendra's household, built in this fashion on his betrayal of his friendship, could not possibly settle down into a happy, loving family; Tagore's sense of poetic justice requires him and his wife Asha to pass through tears of shame, separation and distress. It would have been possible, however, to have the disaster brought about through Bihari, a move that Tagore, obviously, refused to make. Once Mahendra had been established as an impulsive young man acting under the spell of passion, Tagore had to set up a counterpoint manifesting self-denial and loving restraint. Between these two principles represented by two male friends, there was space for Asha and Binodini to play their feminine roles.

Tagore's later elaboration on the types of women (as in his novella *Dui Bon* "Two Sisters") – grouping them under two rubrics, either "showers of the rainy season" (women who soothe, nourish and serve men) or "flowers of springtime" (those who charm, inspire and distract men) – was yet to be formulated when he wrote *Chokher Bali*. It is possible that at that juncture in his writing Tagore was taking the stand that the woman who inspires and tempts can also nourish and serve, after having her intense emotions purged, if a man compatible with her talents is available. Asha as a person of sweet and subdued charm indeed corresponds to the "showers of the rainy season" category (if we may anachronistically bring Tagore's later descriptions to bear on the fictional material of 1902), though her abilities as a woman offering services are somewhat limited. Binodini, as a woman of obvious beauty, talent and warmth, had more potential, if other ways of handling the plot were to be considered.

Whether Tagore ever believed in the possibility of any of his characters experiencing great love within the confines of the household for any length of time is, of course, an open question. His apprehension about stormy passion is more than obvious. Binodini proves a friend to Asha not so much at the early stage, when she helps Asha to write passionate love-letters to Mahendra, as when she eventually removes herself from their household. This home is thus saved by the care and presence of Bihari (Mahendra's friend) who serves the dual purpose of holding Binodini back from Mahendra's life, not mechanically or by force, but by virtue of his power to attract Binodini, and because he is able to attend to the needs of the friend's family when Mahendra needs the help most though he never admits it to himself. Asha's home is also saved by Binodini's decision to move away.

In Tagore's novella *Nashtaneed* ("Broken Nest", the fictional basis of Satyajit Ray's well-known film *Charulata*), Charulata's home could not have been saved in a similar fashion, for it was her own passion that had brought about the disequilibrium. Passion, once aroused, has to work its way through, Tagore had observed in real life. His fiction repeatedly makes the point that one has to wait until the devastation is over and come out purified, if one is strong enough. Charulata has no women friends; her only friend, Amal, turns into an enemy when his presence rouses her passionate desire which her absent-minded husband Bhupati – Amal's elder brother – is incapable of responding to.

Tagore does not appear to blame Bhupati at all for his failure; on the contrary, while presenting Bhupati's innermost thoughts, Tagore is engaged in developing a theory of *economy in love* in conjugal life. His theory suggests that all-consuming love, charming and colourful, is neither necessary nor desirable for our daily lives. Household duties or, duties in general – valuable because useful – can be performed with a minimum of care and loving compassion; these ordinary feelings may have originated in frustrated or sublimated passion, but one should accept gracefully what comes one's way without inquiring where it comes from. There is no reason to regret the fact that great love cannot be sustained in the arena of public action or within the privacy of domestic walls. The best is reserved for the truly secret interior space where silence reigns supreme.

This idea of a secret interior space found beautiful expression in Tagore's musical compositions marked by folk-tunes, and most notably by those of the *baul*s of Bengal. It is in his songs that Tagore appears to take love beyond human boundaries. Many of his songs of separation and waiting, classified in the standard taxonomy of his music as love-songs, could just as well have been labelled as songs of personal devotion, and vice versa. Devotion can be seen as offering a way out to human beings restricted otherwise by an oppressive marriage or other forms of social bondage. Tagore was keenly aware of the power of love to break through the rigid frame of social existence marked by fear, greed and cruelty. The character Nandini in his play *Raktakarabi* (Red Oleanders), celebrates this love as an assertion of life – its force blended with tenderness. She speaks of her beloved Ranjan as an undaunted, ever-green spirit of youthful courage; it is the vigour her body and soul share with him that makes her throb with love; but in his tragic death, a martyr killed by the oppressive regime, Ranjan gives her even greater strength as she resolves to break the obscene hold of the dead over the living, the unjust rule of barbaric and uncomprehending mechanical performance of duty crushing the living joy of nature. Nandini is a depiction of love, but she is not a woman capable of devouring passion.

One would conjecture that Tagore had deep misgivings about the power of passionate love; but he forcefully portrayed it in his mature years in the form of Prakriti (the name literally means "nature") – an untouchable girl in his dance drama *Chandalika* based on a tale from the Buddhist Jātakas. The figure of Prakriti remains darkly magical until she realizes her potential for giving:

> ***Prakriti***: No, nothing shall remain. That is my one wish – that I have the chance to give, to pour out my being and be fulfilled. That is the consummation I have been waiting for. The world has conspired to make me forget what I *can* give. Now I know and I *shall* give – everything that I have![13]

---

13 "Chandalika", Chakravarty, op. cit., p. 173.

In her passionate love Prakriti breaks the barrier of untouchability which held her captive in the unspeakably oppressive framework of the caste regime; but that is all that happens. "Prakriti" (nature, signifying woman) becomes able to come closer to "Ananda" ("divine bliss", the name of the disciple of Buddha she falls in love with) only when she attains the realization that natural pain mingles with divine yearning at the point at which she can welcome him in the perfect, joyful freedom that the name "Ananda" conveys. Prakriti must grant this freedom to Ananda voluntarily, with grace and gratitude, to make him eternally blissful.

Womanly love in Tagore's work stands for a gift – a gift of life, a gift of freedom which may mean death. It is to the woman capable of giving such a present that her beloved acknowledges an indebtedness that overflows all reckoning: "In love I pay my endless debt to thee/for what thou art".[14]

Men and women in contemporary Bengal enjoy the love-songs of Tagore; his dance-dramas are even appreciated elsewhere in India. However, the prevailing atmosphere in most conjugal lives is closer to what is memorably documented in Tagore's poems in his 1890 collection *Manasi* – the sad resentment of the woman and the resigned frustration of the man. Couples today, much as in the poem *Emon diney tarey bala jay* (On a day like this, one can tell her),[15] try to find a moment, suitably darkened by the monsoon clouds, when it becomes fleetingly possible to utter the message of love to the one who will be lost in the petty humdrum existence of everyday obligations as soon as the rains are over. This is not to suggest that contemporary couples would do well to read

---

[14] "Fireflies", Chakravarty, op. cit., p. 340.

[15] [***Editor's note***: The reference is to the 1889 poem "Barshar diney" ("On a Rainy Day", included in the collection *Manasi*), *Rabindra Rachanavali*, Calcutta: Visva-Bharati, vol. 2, 1939, pp. 248-50.]

Manasi every now and then; the point is that the idea of romantic love had not changed much since the turn of the century. But the way spouses today deal with their lives together raises a more basic question: does "love" in contemporary Indian usage bear any resemblance to the "romantic" idea of love?

Complications arise when the question is discussed in a feminist perspective that is confident about the identity and aspirations of "women" in India and elsewhere. Tagore's romantic novel *Shesher Kobita* (The Last Poem), when it appeared, was truly inspiring to young people in love, although many literary critics regarded the book as Tagore's commentary on urban male middle-class Anglophiles in twentieth-century Bengal who frequently betrayed the women who loved them. This idea of "betrayal" in love, which is consistent with the views about failure in love expressed by the discussants in my group conversations reported earlier, is not quite in keeping with Tagore's theory of love, which is Romantic but set in a different perspective. His heroine Labanya, who is capable of love of the "overflowing" kind and can "fill the void" with her infinite and affectionate loving, is not someone of whom one might meaningfully say that a lover had "betrayed" her. If one roots for Katy/Ketaki and pleads on her behalf (as Labanya does, in the novel), then one is in fact getting trapped in Tagore's dichotomy of manly love vs. womanly love, which is unacceptable to feminists in general.

Tagore's approach to the matter was relatively nuanced: he was aware of the androgynous character of human identity and its implications for the question of love.[16] It is true that he kept harping on what he took to be the essential differences between men and women, and that he found it difficult to

[16] *Chithipatra* [selected correspondence], vol. 9, Calcutta: Visva-Bharati, 1954, passim.

revise his belief that love comes in two varieties, feminine and masculine. In his novel *Ghare-Baire* (Home and the World), for instance, he has a minor female character advise Vimala that, while a man must have addictions of some sort, she should take care that he does not get addicted to a woman. However, this strand of his thinking is taken less seriously by feminists, who prefer to remember Tagore as the creator of such a figure as Chitrangada. As he portrays her, Chitrangada initially experiences the agony of having her love rejected in a way that puts her human dignity at stake, but later succeeds in regaining her personal sense of worth by willingly renouncing the feminine beauty that she had on loan from the god of love (Madana) for a year.[17] Chitrangada is a celebration of joyful womanly love blended with personal accountability and self-respect. Another text that feminists value is *Streer Patra* (A Letter from a Wife), a short story in which Tagore explicitly asserts the human rights of women. In his narratives the claim to these rights, however, sometimes undergoes displacement, forcing the story to end in death or in surrender to a personal deity – Tagore often invokes Mīrābāī in this context. These moves in his writing makes his approach to "women's rights" elusive to many women readers today; what stands out with less ambiguity is Tagore's spontaneous appreciation of women as he writes:

> Bring beauty and order into my forlorn life, woman, as you brought them into my house when you lived./Sweep away the dusty fragments of the hours, fill the empty jars, and mend all that has been neglected./Then open the inner door of the shrine, light the candle, and let us meet in silence before our God."[18]

---

17 A well-known adaptation of the *Mahābhārata* episode of Arjuna (in exile) marrying the crown princess of Manipur; they had a son, Babhruvāhana. Tagore's *Chitrangada*, initially a play in blank verse, was eventually rewritten by him as a full-fledged dance-drama.

18 "From *Fruit-Gathering*", Chakravarty, op. cit., p. 321.

This is then the point at which humanity, irrespective of the sex of the body or the gender assigned to it by society's grammatical code, meet in perfect harmony, at the inner altar of God, and remain united eternally, in Tagore's view.

(Sri) Aurobindo begins to speak of love both physical and spiritual in less ambiguous terms but eventually takes a mystical turn in his use of legends and myths.

Born to a family in which the forces of Westernization and those of the self-asserting Indian patriotic spirit had been pulling the children in different directions, Aurobindo was more at ease with the English language while expressing his intense dedication to Mother India. His 1895 collection of poems indicates his competence and willingness to emerge as a European poet. This willingness appears to have persisted all through his life even when in his later years he was engaged in the process of composing his epic poem *Savitri*. In his discursive prose writings he acknowledged this general willingness – though indirectly – in the form of an analysis of the presence of external influence in contemporary Indian culture. The following excerpts from his writing indicate why he did not follow the lead of Michael Madhusudan Datta (1824-73) who like him began his creative writings in the medium of English but who later became a major Bengali poet.

In his analysis, Aurobindo criticizes the "attempt in the last century which still in some directions continues (. . .) to make ourselves a sort of Brown Englishmen" but pointed out that

> a certain amount of imitation, a great amount even, was (. . .) a psychological necessity of the situation (. . .) a certain amount of acceptance of forms too, – some imitation, if all taking over of forms must be called imitation, – is inevitable. (. . .). The question is what we do with them and whether we can bring them to be instruments and by some characteristic

modification moulds of our own spirit.[19]

Several decades after his passing, critics agree that Aurobindo did successfully deploy the Western model (of writing poetry) as an instrument that fully expressed his articulation of "our own spirit", the spirit of his "motherland".

As we re-examine this process, we have the option of seeing his engagement as a method of establishing the supremacy of a mother-figure (embodied in the meaning and spirit of the content) over a father-figure (manifested as the form of the language); in real life, it was his father who made him accept the primacy of the English language in his formative years. The way Aurobindo adored his motherland was also different from Michael Madhusudan Dutt's style (exemplified in the latter's well-known farewell note, his poem "To the Motherland"[20]); Aurobindo kept himself free from tender-minded sentimentality. He found his model in Bankimchandra Chatterjee (1838-94), in whose writing the figure of the Mother stood for power and resourcefulness (the iconic place where this is articulated is the song "Vande Mataram" composed by Bankim). Aurobindo shared this view with Bankim.

Bankim's depiction of women – both as bearers of naturalness, as representatives of Nature herself (as in the novel *Kapalakundala* and its eponymous heroine), and as selfless performers of household chores, free from attachment and

---

19 Sri Aurobindo, *The Foundations of Indian Culture* [this passage is quoted from *The Complete Works*, vol. 20, 1997 edn., pp. 45-46].

20 [***Editor's note***: The reference is to the sonnet "Bangabhumir prati" (To Bengal); although its title does not project Bengal as a mother, the entire poem does, starting from the very first line *rekho ma daserey money, e minoti kori padey* (Mother, do keep this servant in mind, I fall on your feet and implore you); an English rendering is available in Ghulam Murshid, 2003, *Lured by Hope: A Biography of Michael Madhusudan Dutt*, London: Oxford University Press, p. 156.]

anxieties – entertained and inspired a culturally diverse range of readers in the nineteenth century. His application of the principles of the *Gītā* in these literary depictions within the framework of the social mores of his time no doubt represented his understanding of how those principles could be presented vividly and concretely to his readers; but Aurobindo, otherwise attracted to Bankim's approach, placed the *Gītā* in a national (and spiritual) perspective within the framework of his heroic-poetic vision; his writings that referred to the *Gītā* paid no direct attention to the narrow confines of Indian domesticity. Aurobindo did not share Bankim's analysis; love's progress from the conjugal life through several phases culminating in the love of God (as shown in Bankim's novel *Krishnakanter Will*) had no place in Aurobindo's scheme of things. Aurobindo's idea of *love* developed in its contrast to *death*. Life asserts itself over death through its power of love. Death, with its negative presence, only enhances the love of life, and of the living. This poetic vision of love asserting life against Death could have taken a romantic form in Aurobindo's later writings; we can counterfactually imagine a course of conceptual development associating his spiritual message of life-affirmation with the beauty of literary portrayals of the way love develops in interpersonal contexts. But the way Aurobindo did in fact develop his vision of love led in a different direction, illustrated by the statement

> (. . .) that the Mother will ere the end have done her work and made the very earth of thy being a joy and a purity.[21]

Aurobindo's idea of love as a movement of vital energy ascending upwards found a natural place in his conceptualization of the Life Divine. As he saw it, life was evolving through various levels of consciousness and thus had in it the

---

[21] Sri Aurobindo, *Thoughts and Aphorisms* [this passage is quoted from *The Complete Works*, vol. 12, 1997 edn., p. 461, aphorism 279].

potential to replicate divinity: "When will the world change into the model of heaven?" he asks, and answers –

> When all mankind becomes boys & girls together with God revealed as Krishna & Kali, the happiest boy & strongest girl of the crowd, playing together in the gardens of Paradise.

In this spiritual mystical representation, he speaks of every variety of love (of man, of woman, of things) as "the love of God reflected in these living images". Aurobindo decries "reason", which "receives the impulse subconsciously"; he claims that when reason "pretends to originate or impel, it is masking other agencies".[22]

One of the distinctive strands in Aurobindo's thinking is his thesis that action invokes the principle of the Mother, who stands for an inextricable unity of thought and effort; without the Mother, there is no action. This notion is in conformity with the theme that our folk wisdom shares with some schools of scriptural thinking and leads to the tendency to describe the Goddess as *Icchāmayī* (the willful one), the very category of Will/Desire incarnate in the feminine principle. In Aurobindo's words:

> the divine Shakti not only inspires and guides, but initiates and carries out your works; all your movements are originated by her (. . .). There can be no more happy condition than this union and dependence.[23]

Even in this appreciation of the joy and the purity in the union with the Mother, however, Aurobindo does not forget the temptress; he suggests "two ways of avoiding the snare of women; one is to shun all women and the other to love all beings".[24] In the space marked by this love for "all beings"

---

22 Sri Aurobindo, *Thoughts and Aphorisms* [pp. 490-91; pp. 458-59].

23 Sri Aurobindo, *The Mother* [this passage is quoted from *The Complete Works*, vol. 32, 1997 edn., pp. 12-13].

24 Sri Aurobindo, *Thoughts and Aphorisms* [this passage is quoted from *The Complete Works*, vol. 12, 1997 edn., p. 463, aphorism 304].

and the active love associated with the divine Mother, Aurobindo's *Savitri* is not a bridge connecting these ideas; she encompasses love in all its forms, defined and undefined.

In the poetic narration of love's battle against death that ends with death surrendering, Aurobindo clearly locates the life-generating principle (Mother) in Sāvitrī – a name carrying distinct meanings in various contexts in the Purāṇas and the epics. Sāvitrī in the *Ṛgveda* is a prayer, also called Gāyatrī,[25] addressed to *Savitṛ* or the Sun. Tagore's poem *Savitri* invokes this association and at the same time touches upon the idea of the energy that generates life and keeps it pulsating in a particular body. It is possible to argue that Aurobindo chooses the Sāvitrī figure of the *Mahābhārata* as she keeps the life of her beloved Satyavān flowing into a new generation against the forces of time (Kāla). She, as the Mother, generates life within the limits of mortality, for mortality assures the uninterrupted evolution in progress enabling the creation of new forms – elevating life, and love, to higher levels.

Aurobindo's *Savitri* introduces herself to Death in the following words:

> world-spirit, I was thy equal spirit born/My will too is a law, my strength a god./I am immortal in my mortality.[26]

Rebutting Death's reasoning she says,

> Reason that scans and breaks, but cannot build/Or builds in vain because she doubts her work./I am, I love, I see, I act, I will.[27]

Before his final surrender Death is given a full view of Śakti

---

[25] Monier Williams, 1827, *Sanskrit–English Dictionary*, Oxford: Clarendon Press, p. 287, c. 2.

[26] Sri Aurobindo, *Savitri: A Legend and a Symbol* [this passage is quoted from *The Complete Works*, vols. 33-34, 1997 edn., p. 589].

[27] Ibid. [p. 594].

(the Mother) as embodied in Sāvitrī. This notion of a loving will is not one that immediately reaches the average reader, for such readers tend to be certain that they know what is involved when they "live" and "act" in real life, and that they need no supplement to their naive certainty. Contemporary men and women in India, whose suffering often focuses on the thought of being "betrayed" in love, are yet to reach the stage at which

> Love is not the heart's hunger for affection,/Love is a mighty vibration coming straight from the one, and only the very pure and very strong are capable of receiving and manifesting it.[28]

This utterance by the Mother, in the Aurobindo Ashram's *Bulletin*, articulates for a wider audience Aurobindo's "insistence on the rejection of all untransformed vital movements", his distinction between "the world-movement of sex" and an appropriately transformed "vital" movement.

The general run of men and women not yet thus transformed usually regard Yogīs and Mothers as cult figures. When one observes the people who rush to ashrams, one finds that many of them, in their personal lives, are "failures" in love. In their everyday actions, ordinary people, depending on the received wisdom, think of men and women as being like "fire" and "ghee", which must be kept apart to avoid accidents. An easy way to handle this "difficulty" is found in marriage. Once marriage is viewed as a medicine designed to prevent, or to cure, the "problems" of love, its source of validity is devalued. Surely one should expect married couples to experience the bliss of conjugal love and the love of children; the stereotype-laden approach that reduces it to problem-solving also undermines this love.

Where does Aurobindo stand? He appears to place marital

---

28 The Mother, *Bulletin*, November 1963, p. 25.

existence under the rubric of the "world-movement of sex", leaving his visualization of the interpersonal life of a couple less clearly articulated than one might wish. The "harmony" invoked in his formulations, while its cosmic dimensions are made explicit, is specified at the level of human individuals as a spiritual state of the "soul", leaving open – no doubt to be worked out by different couples differently, without direct guidance from his writings – what this can concretely mean for soul-mates seeking a meaningful partnership between two co-evolving adults.

4

Myths, Rules and Romantic Devotion

TAGORE'S approach to the riddle of the co-existence of the ascetic and the erotic in the figure of Śiva led him, especially in the words of his songs, to the poetic image of a Naṭarāja playing out the rhythmic succession of seasons and other alternating natural phenomena in his eternal dance. Tagore's image derives some of its potency from the ambivalence of the term *kāla* – meaning both "time" and "death" – in the standard Bengali terms for the seasons, such as *Vasantakāla* (spring-time) or *Śaratkāla* (autumn-time). The ascetic summer, with its heat (*tāpa*) of *tapasyā*, appears full of wrath; this mood of nature's is subdued by the monsoon's showering tenderness, and attains fulfilment with arrival of autumn with its pure, childlike beauty. This beauty vanishes, however, when winter appears to subject the earth to dreadful austerity and deprivation; but this turns out to have been a prelude to the re-asserted glory and expansive beauty of nature in spring. What makes spring vibrant is the clarity of the dance of life and death; spring celebrates arrivals and departures at once; there is parity, Tagore's songs suggest, between the dry leaves and faded flowers that are cleared away and the equally abundant new leaves and blossoms bursting into vitality. In his lightly written dialogue-format essays in his early book *Panchabhuta* (The Five Elements), Tagore granted death a certain supremacy over the material world. The exuberant creative writings of his later years, which sing in praise of the rhythmically pulsating dance of natural renewal through the ever repeated cycle of seasons, may perhaps be interpreted as a recantation of his earlier view of death.

While Tagore's choosing to associate Śiva's cosmic dance with the terrestrial seasonal cycle is his own, his references to the androgynous presentation of Śiva (as "Pārvatī-Parameśvara") draw on the classical tradition. Nowhere in his innumerable references to Śiva, however, does Tagore ever invoke the phallus as a symbol of Śiva; it is possible that he ascribed that symbolism to tribal origins, as he did in the case of Kālī, Cāmuṇḍā and similar forms of Śakti, the feminine principle. It is hard to ascertain if it is uneasiness about such tribal associations that explains his silence about the myth of Paraśurāma – the well-known matricide (this story appears in the Śānti-Parva of *Mahābhārata*) who is also seen as the founder of the virgin land of Kerala. For Tagore is not alone; this powerful myth seems to have been neglected by most thinkers and creative artists. While the myth of Yayāti has attracted the attention of modern Indian playwrights, that of Viṣṇu's sixth *avatāra* Paraśurāma – a favourite of Bengal's folk theatre in the 1930s (although the emphases in that interpretation were a bit quirky) – is yet to be seriously reinterpreted in contemporary terms.

Tagore's reinterpretation of characters from several Indian myths and epics is one vehicle conveying his sense of the cultural striving that is obligatory for all of us; he takes it that a person unscathed by civilization has not even begun the journey to self-realization on which one becomes a full-fledged human being. His stated preference for Rāma of the epic (as a model for the ego-ideal of his Bengali readers) over against Kr̥ṣṇa as portrayed in the Vaiṣṇava tradition is a case in point. Tagore prefers Rāma the righteous, who embodies the *law*. Rāma not only follows his father's implicit commands: he almost personifies the Word of the Father, the category of the promise as the repository of truth; his actions have the effect of breaking the heart of his actual terrestrial father, who dies. That this dimension of the narrative does not diminish Tagore's appreciation of Rāma suggests that he accepts the Western view of culture at the level of structures, rules and reasoning based on the truth or falsity of verbalizations. Kṛṣṇa, the flute-playing boy symbolizing the intense and innocent charm of first love, cannot possibly be valorised in this frame of reference. Rādhā, however, does gain entry into the world of his poetry, bringing in her trail the evocative association of the River Yamunā, her longing for Kṛṣṇa's flute-playing and the entire narrative that Tagore's notion of righteousness sets aside at a normative level. Had Tagore written at length about feminine power in active contexts in the social space, he might conceivably have invoked the figure of Rādhā with her capacity for infinite suffering. But his world of poetry admittedly remained distant from the realm of action where he wanted to valorise a different love, one blended with the strength for work. A love disconnected from that strength would not flourish; it would turn into a stagnant emotion that led nowhere.[1]

As we try today to understand this emphasis on order, rules, method, we may adopt the working hypothesis that Tagore, like many other thinkers and visionaries of the nineteenth century, had a particular goal in mind: he was engaged in reviewing every aspect of life stretched over the social arena in search of a leading principle unifying all actions under a common purpose. The way of life habitually followed by people all around him looked so pointless and wasteful that he felt his people had to regain a sense of purpose; he

---

[1] Tagore's poem "Shahjahan" [*Rabindra Rachanavali*, vol. 12, Calcutta: Visva-Bharati, 1942, pp. 14-20] addresses this binary of love and an individual's life. Love, or at least some of its great moments, can perhaps be permanently monumentalized in a memorial like the Taj Mahal, Tagore writes; but life goes on.

shared this quest with Bankim, Vivekananda and Aurobindo. Such a unifying principle could not be provided by emotional ties. Love in the mode of sweet romance leads nowhere;[2] and yet a poet like Tagore could not but assert the power of love. He also felt the attraction of nature, which he expressed in his poems, his fiction, his discursive prose, his paintings, his music. Culture enables human beings to preserve that which is natural, spontaneous and tender, by cherishing and carefully protecting women and children – inarticulate, subdued, secret, precious assets. Does this view of the enterprise of culture reconcile what Tagore saw as the requirements of the unifying principle of active partnership with fellow actors with the need to recognize the unique worth of the natural and the spontaneous?

There is a contrast between his songs, where Tagore glorifies the idea of the immeasurably valuable feminine presence, and his dance drama *Chitrangada*, which reaffirms the inner demands of "culture". Arjuna was eager to meet the brave princess of Manipur and take part in her heroic battle against armed invaders before he came to recognize the beautiful maiden in his arms as none other than the princess. After this recognition, however, the promised "friendship" between Arjuna and Citrāṅgadā never materializes, for as the world of action (visualized in terms of the rule-governed notion of culture) would have it, Citrāṅgadā must stay on to take care of the baby who is about to be born, while Arjuna must depart to carry out his various missions. In this representation, Citrāṅgadā also stands for the force of culture; even though initially she performs her "natural" function by

[2] There is a nursery rhyme in Bengali – *dhonke niye bonke jabo, sekhane khabo ki?/nirale bosia chander mukh nirokhi* (I'll take my darling to the woods; and what are we to eat there?/I'll sit in solitude and look at the face of my little moon) – expressing a thought applicable to grown-up darlings as well.

switching on a god-given charming exterior to attract Arjuna, eventually she asserts her truth, her higher nature as a cultured human being, by disavowing this external charm and revealing herself as the princess-warrior that she really is. That revelation promises a friendship that the culture does not let them consummate.

This unfulfilled expectation of friendship between men and women did not become a matter of concern in any milieu during the nineteenth or the early twentieth century, for a deep skepticism about the possibility of heterosexual friendship has persisted everywhere. Kr̥ṣṇa's friendship with Draupadī (whose "real" name was Kr̥ṣṇā; Draupadī merely means "Drupada's daughter") narrated in the *Mahābhārata* has never been chosen as a theme for serious elite writing present or past; it has had no takers in the oral or folk theatre traditions either. Has it found any takers at all? What are Aurobindo's views, for example?

Aurobindo, in his discourse on *yoga*, admitted the theoretical possibility of friendship between men and women, provided they were alert "that the lower vital should not look in at the back door";[3] Aurobindo, like other authors, is silent on the friendship between Kr̥ṣṇa and Kr̥ṣṇā a.k.a. Draupadī. We could conceivably read Tagore's *Chitrangada* as hinting at the possibility of true friendship between men and women –

---

[3] Retrieved on 18 July 2014 at the URL http://www.sriaurobindoashram.com/Content.aspx?ContentURL=_staticcontent/sriaurobindoashram/-09%20e-library/-01%20Works%20of%20Sri%20Aurobindo/-01%20English/-02_Other%20Editions/Letters%20of%20Sri%20Aurobindo/-01_First%20Series%201947/-09_The%20True%20Foundation%20of%20Love%20.htm

[***Editor's Note***: The passage quoted in the text occurs in section VI, *Love: Human to Divine*, specifically, in Aurobindo's letter dated 7 July 1936 published under the heading "Friendship and psychic love".]

one would imagine that such examples might inspire young people in India if their social milieu were to provide the possibility of concrete projects where they can jointly conceptualize and implement plans of their own. It should be clear that merely "working together" in institutional settings created by forces over which they have no individual control does not amount to a context in which friendship, as a crucible within which projects can be incubated, becomes fully meaningful in its own terms.

In the context of our study, understanding *Chitrangada* involves re-examining the way Tagore's Chitrangada figure represents the idea of love. A contemporary critic of his, Dwijendra Lal Roy (1863–1913), a major dramatist and composer in his own right, severely criticized Tagore for writing a play like this, given the fact that the moral code of India does not permit any "decent" woman to come forward freely to make an offer of love.

That it was possible for Roy to brush aside Chitrangada's association with the epic tradition – free from the injunctions of the Book of Manu that became prevalent in later times – indicates the heightening of tension arising out of cultural, intellectual and moral conflicts besetting India under British rule. The distinction between a "decent" and an "indecent" woman/man emerged forcefully at this juncture of our social life – and of commentary, including literary criticism – on the basis of a historical fact, the earlier acceptance of *Manu Saṁhitā* (the Book of Manu) as the normative code of social conduct in Hindu society. Codifying normative rules serves to divide the population into those who are law-abiding, "decent", and those who violate the rules and "indecently" resist control. Poetry and myth permit vagueness at the boundaries; a book of law is not designed to do so. Where did Manu stand on women?

The Book of Manu stresses the need to keep "sisters, wives,

daughters and all girls who are wedded into the family"[4] happy to bring prosperity to the family and the clan. By implication those who fall outside the range of kinship ties are banished from the entitlement of happiness and care; in other words, they are disgraced. It is interesting that mothers are not mentioned in the list, presumably because mothers need to have no happiness arranged for them – surely the Mother *is* care and happiness personified; she is glorious; it is in her image that women are glorified. Manu says that women deserve the highest respect because they graciously add children to the clan and bring grace and brightness to the home; his formulation banishes Rādhā from the world of "respectable" women.

It is not easy to see how any serious thinker in the formative decades of modern Indian social inquiry could have tried to harmonize the laws in the Book of Manu with the idea of feminine power, Śakti, which is a major strand in India's civilizational heritage. Manu does elaborately codify, in the form of *sannyāsa*, what many anthropologists (and others) see as a way out of the restrictive rules that Indian society imposed on individuals who wanted to be different. The Book of Manu, however, is unable to assign a valid place to, and thus cannot handle in its system, female (or male) performers/courtesans, who neither fit the social roles specified in the code nor opt out as *sannyāsins*. A conceptually elegant solution to this predicament might have taken the form of considering all public women as "wives" of the king and all such men as his servants, whereupon the king, discharging his duties as the ruler of the land and its people, would have proceeded to keep them happy. This kind of speculation need not hold our attention. The point we do need to note is that, as long as

---

[4] Hirendranath Datta, 1970, *Manur Varnashramadharma*, Calcutta: Jadavpur University. [Datta completed the manuscript in 1942, shortly before his death.]

women are regarded as possessions to be "looked after" by some ruler, they are not seen having any force or Śakti of their own.

India has had this problem ever since Manu became the authority on social relations (including questions of gender in particular) while the myth of Śakti as the prime mover of the world of events continued to shape people's thoughts both at level of folk beliefs and in the upper strata of society, whose theoreticians tried to solve the riddle by drawing on the philosophical doctrines of the Sāṁkhya school. The Śākta interpretation struck a compromise: the Goddess (Durgā) comes over to Rāma's side when he propitiates her with untimely, unusual *pūjā* to ask for her aid in his battle with Rāvaṇa, a devotee of Śaṅkara (and by implication of Śaṅkara–Pārvatī as a divine couple). The ritual of Devī-Pūjā at the time of Dussehra requires a handful of earth from the doorstep of fallen women, because the latter, in their labour of offering pleasure to everyone, in perfect joy and freedom, are viewed in this tradition as manifesting Bhagavatī. This dreaded and sacred power of women, inarticulately valorised by common people in eastern India (and in the coastal regions all the way to southern India as well), has little relevance for Manu, whose codification reflects straightforward patriarchy.

These incongruous elements came to the surface and gave rise to anomalies when many of our significant thinkers who played a formative role in modern Indian culture wanted to invoke the Mother and yet remain true to the laws of Manu. The problem with old myths structured and restructured through generations of common people is that they cannot easily serve as instruments for such purposes. Sri Aurobindo's references to the Mother – often equating the feminine power with "soul-power" – mystifies ordinary persons who express their own version in a simple statement like "The mother has an exalted position in India; she is higher than heaven." This type of statement evokes a sentiment universally appreciated but not analysed. The apparent synthesis it brings about in practical social life is also of dubious value, as has been shown in my earlier references to Bankim's treatment of mother's love in his narratives.[5]

Aurobindo's acceptance of Bankim's *Vande Mataram*, affirming his faith and commitment to the service of the sacred motherland, was a way of blending power with love for the mother. In their project of fighting for the freedom of the motherland, the young men of India did forge ties of friendship; the years of the nationalist movement were not marked by constant interventions of the Father. And yet it became clear that many of these young men did feel the urge to find a *guru*, a father-substitute, who would lead them in their secret mission. They often found this *guru* in one of the key figures, a big brother whose charisma held the group together. Tagore was openly enthusiastic about ties of friendship,[6] but not about elevating someone to the status of a *guru*. Furthermore, the idea of the motherland asking for the blood of martyrs to secure freedom had little appeal for Tagore, who was a true believer in love for mankind in a universal frame of reference. The world of work as he visualized it would flourish in a climate of joyful effort without the rigour of discipline or punishment. He felt confident that, if everything in the natural world could work through uniformly law-abiding processes, without having to have any external agency imposing law and order, there was no reason

---

[5] Cf. my "Matri-Rupena", *Samaj-Mon*, Calcutta: Firma KLM, 1977 [repr. in Manashi Dasgupta, *Samaj-Mon o Nari-Bhashya*, Kolkata: Samatat, 2011].

[6] Tagore's well-known song on "Raksha-bandhan" (*Banglar mati, Banglar jal, Banglar bayu* [. . .] *punya hok hey Bhagaban* – "God, may the soil, the water, the winds. . . of Bengal be consecrated") may be recalled in this context.

why human beings should fail to achieve optimal self-expression through work – especially in India, where there was once a rich and durable heritage of harmony between humans, other living beings and the energies of Nature. This unimposed order was what he tried to bring about through the way of love and friendliness at his ashram in Santiniketan, whose air was alive with his songs and discourses for years.

Tagore's preferred route of escape from the bondage of rules was music and the fine arts. In his recreation of Citrāṅgadā's love it is possible to hear a resonance of Rādhā's yearning superbly expressed by one of his favourite Vaiṣṇava poets, Chandidas: *Soi, kebaa sunaailo syaama naam* ("my friend, who (first) said the name of Śyāma in my presence?" – the poem continues as follows: "The sound of his name pierced my heart and left me restless"); restless love is uniquely identified with Rādhā in the Indian context. Sītā is a virtuous wife, so the story goes, but Rādhā *is* love; love in its purest form is *parakīyā* (love with *someone else's* woman), as remarked by a major Bengali writer.[7] The rules, obviously, prohibit this; as a consequence, love is *taboo* in Indian *society*; as a further consequence, love becomes *sacred* in the *culture*.

Scholarly interpreters of Vaiṣṇava treatises and *padas* (poetry) took the Rādhā–Kr̥ṣṇa lore, and the idea of *parakīyā* love, in a spiritual direction, making Rādhā a symbol for the human soul held in thraldom in the material world. Caitanya's emergence between the fifteenth and the sixteenth century as a saint who had started out as a scholar elaborating this interpretation made it a culturally iconic construal; to his devotees, Caitanya was and remains Kr̥ṣṇa, the dark god, reborn in Gaurāṅga, a fair-skinned Rādhā-body. That

7 Annadasankar Ray, 1976, *Prem o Bandhuta* ("Love and friendship", Kolkata: Banishilpa, title essay pp. 3-15). Author's file copy received through the kindness and courtesy of Lila Ray and Annadasankar Ray.

Gaurāṅga, on entering the stage of *sannyāsa*, chose the name Caitanya (consciousness), had three purposes:

1. to experience Rādhā's exalted love;
2. through this experience, to reach the immeasurably joyous Śrī Kṛṣṇa; and
3. to realize divine Rādhā's ecstasy by merging these experiences.[8]

This blissful state, of course, had to be attained through a body, a human form purified not through the performance of any ritual but by love and the chanting of the name of Hari (Kṛṣṇa). The renewal of *bhakti* (devotion), under the leadership of Caitanya and other *bhakta*s, was a movement of dissent against caste rituals and religious exclusiveness. Caitanya fervently believed in the power of personal faith and devotion; from his life and preaching emerged a formulation that has literally become a proverb in Bengali, *bishwase milaye krishna, tarke bahu dur* (faith takes you to Kṛṣṇa; rational debate takes far too long).

Early Vaiṣṇavism inculcated a practice of praying to Kṛṣṇa as one's son/lover/friend, with faith in a God who would respond to all these forms of adoration. Caitanya's movement reinforced the tradition of emotive devotion, the quest for salvation through chanting the name of God to the rhythm of one's dancing body. This faith presupposed propositional beliefs whose validity would not be amenable to rational scrutiny. Caste leaders and authority figures in society have always had reasons to be unhappy about such movements. The strength of the renewed Vaiṣṇava movement however lay in the utter humility of Caitanya and his associates. The disarming humility preached and practised by the followers of this group keeps the movement going in eastern India to this day in several forms.

The specific anguish of Caitanya's "Kṛṣṇa-consciousness"

---

[8] Kanti P. Datta, 1957, *Gaur-Katha*, Calcutta: Rajendra Library, pp. 24-25.

(an English term recently coined by certain devotees based in the West) and his acceptance of the body make his style of devotion quite distinct from what has been observed in similarly inspired devotees of the past, such as Mīrābāī. Mīrābāī was a devotee, and a composer of memorable songs, in whose faith romantic yearning was blended with devotion. When Mīrābāī sings: *hari vinā kyuṁ jivam re maiṅ* (How can I possibly live without Hari?),[9] she reminds us of the early Vaiṣṇava poet Vidyāpati who, speaking on behalf of Rādhā, writes:

> How do I spend entire days and nights without Hari? It is raining heavily, in the month of Bhadra, and my temple is empty.

This ideal romance, narrated and sung over the centuries all over India, in several languages, features the ever-elusive divine beloved, and the woman overflowing with a love that human embraces can never consummate. The twelfth-century saint Mahādevīyakkā of Karnataka claims herself to be "the woman of love/for my lord, white as jasmine"; addressing her own mother as a confidante she confesses:

> Mother, because they all have thorns/in their chests,/I cannot take/any man in my arms but my lord/white as jasmine.[10]

Mahādevīyakkā, like Mīrābāī and many others, reaches a high peak of spirituality and attains the status of a "*sant*" through love; but society and its groups remain exactly as they had been – full of thorns and poison. Caitanya too remains a riddle and a miracle. The touch of love inspires ordinary men and women, but eludes their reach; their unquenched yearning leads them to yet another Bābā, or Guru – or Mother.

---

9 A.J. Alston (tr.), 1980, *The Devotional Poems of Mirabai*, Delhi: Motilal Banarsidass, p. 141.

10 A.K. Ramanujan (tr.), 1973, *Speaking of Siva*, Harmondsworth: Penguin, repr. 1985, pp. 124-25.

5

Conclusions

FREUD has sometimes been described as a theorist bent on showing that all human achievements could be explained away in terms of a family romance. My effort has been to push the story a little further back and suggest that Freud's theory of libido is actually an attempt to locate the romance within the body of the "protagonist" (the newborn hero of the narrative).[1]

1. In my limited and brief overview of Freud (Chapter 1) I tried to indicate that this suggestion of mine seems to receive support from Lacan's interpretation of Freud. The fact that Freud was a contemporary of Tagore (and of several other nineteenth-century thinkers whose work has shaped modern India) is another important fact noted in that chapter (one that awaits due elaboration in my book based on this report).[2] The exposition of Freud's work in that chapter

---

[1] [***Editor's note***: "Protagonist" is a stopgap; I am not familiar with any English term that would convey what needs to be expressed here. In her discursive texts in Bengali, the author frequently uses *jātaka* (literally "someone born") in the sense of "the individual in question", thus redeploying in serious analytical prose an expression that appears in personal horoscopes to refer to the individual that the horoscope is about – there the term means a "particular individual born under such and such a constellation of influences".]

[2] [***Editor's note***: I chose not to edit out these passages in which the author made it explicit that she intended to expand this project report into a comprehensive study.]

also takes up the idea of narcissistic love coupled with urge to go beyond the limits of bodily pleasures, and discusses his views on the place of the unconscious in the human psyche.

2. My exposition tracks the concept of *desire* in India, beginning with a reference to Buddha's early statements, and focusing on the attachment/ detachment dichotomy invoked, sometimes openly but often implicitly, in other trends of ancient and modern thought. In this part of my discussion, I try to show that Buddha's *bodhi* (enlightenment) consists in freeing the forces of rational deliberation from the *passion* that preoccupies the not yet individuated body of the newborn-attached-to-the-mother. Freud's idea of libidinal attachment to the "self" – that is, the narcissistically constituted self, where lost *objects* are absorbed back into the topography with the aid of the unconscious, helps us to trace the development of the enlightened ego (in the sense that was introduced by Buddha). Buddha finds the lost object of the id (the Mother), takes a close look, confirms that it is gone forever, and emerges from the search, the battle, the inner turmoil, with a decision not to look for the *object* ever again. Buddha's refusal to talk about Immortality, God and other metaphysical issues can be construed as symbolizing his *acceptance* of the loss of and separation from the mother – and from what Freud's detractors call the "family romance". Buddha's conscious resistance against the possibility of the yearning for the mother invading the rational world of action, as well as Buddha's cultivation of a compassion dissociated from its passion-laden roots, acquires special significance in the context of such a reading. I have tried to indicate how Buddhist

rationalism, along with its project of friendship, had to yield to the forces of the mother emerging once again in the culture, with even greater impact on various theories and modes of life.

3. I have offered a panoramic but selective view of thoughts and expressions of love and friendship in India, choosing viewpoints that enable me to emphasize the emergence of modern rational explications of love and friendship, and the reaffirmation of theoretical constructs of the old systems (with innovative content added).

The Hindu societal structure in India, linking sex through marriage to the social obligations of every person born within the fold of the family system, gives marriage a central place of importance in everybody's practical life; and yet, as Chapter 3 shows on the basis of systematically elicited testimony, conjugal life in India is affected by the lack of freedom to let love between a man and his wife grow and flourish. Vivekananda had rightly observed that our marriages are not intended to offer sexual pleasures to men and women. Traditional Indian marriage is indeed an institution designed for social welfare. But Manu (referred to in Chapter 4) sternly warned that keeping the women of the house unhappy and dissatisfied would be perilous for the householder and his clan; likewise, other observers given to thinking and deliberation were able to gauge the depth of unhappiness being generated in a home if marriage were to bring only responsibility and no immediate pleasure to women physically removed from the natal family with whom they had identified, as their "own people", before they got married.

Elaborate treatises on the art of love-making extend implicit recognition to the fact that a husband is in a position to establish the primacy of his claim to his woman over her brother's claim to her loyalty, provided that his amorous charm successfully targets her tender attentions (a terrain prohibited for the brother). It is this success that such treatises propose to guarantee. The aim of love on such a view is to fulfil the needs of the body and rouse it to overflowing pleasure. Men and women incapable of such arousal are also incapable of bringing cheerful cooperativeness to their social responsibilities. Stressing this point is my way of suggesting that all that is erotic is not natural. The body is obviously a product of nature. But one takes serious ownership of one's body through a cultural process, which unavoidably affects the *naturalness* of the human body.

Indian theorists known for their heterodox views were no less interested in the development of cultural values than the orthodox philosophers. Some of the heterodox thinkers supported a culture of eroticism promoting "life-asserting" values – the affirmation of terrestrial life with its full richness – whereas the orthodox schools attached less value to life in this world and preferred to propagate a culture that promises the attainment of higher values to persons who rigorously practise austerity and seek to subjugate the body under the supremacy of the soul. In other words, the orthodox position (here portrayed somewhat abstractly, ignoring certain variations among the schools of thought) remained committed to a version of the dichotomy of *body* and *soul* that regarded the body as opposed to the *soul*, a doctrine that associated higher values exclusively with the soul. Only through the soul which it houses can the body possibly gain access to higher values.

This duality, which of course is also present in Western thought, acquires further complexity in Indian systems, because many subdivisions are introduced in the conceptions of the body, the mind, the soul, with corresponding complications in Indian expositions on love. Thinkers today taking up these issues would do well to look at indeterminacies in ordinary discourse prevalent in contemporary India. Consider a lover experiencing the pangs of separation: where is the love located in the body as normally imaged, and where is the pain felt? The default answer in rural Bengali is "in the liver" (the word is pronounced *kolija, koilja, kolje,* depending on the dialect). Educated urban respondents would be likely to say "in one's heart, in one's heart of hearts", or provide other echoes of widely circulated poetry. Devotees in love with the Godhead who have remained immersed in the poetry of their tradition might say they feel the throbbing of this love "in every limb". This range of variation is distinctive of India. The multiplicity of words for love in Indian languages is also worth observing; it has not yet been studied systematically. Details apart, however, the parallel with the West stands at a general level: the body–mind dualism in the West has doctrinally presided over a trajectory of spiritual, secular, romantic conceptions of love; that itinerary is on the whole comparable to the Indian dualism of body vs. spirit or soul, whose overarching philosophical presence has likewise persisted as a basic architecture around which specific local visualizations of love are articulated, even at the local or folk level.

The earlier phase of Indian systematization of theories of love (and action), when its key concepts were revitalized by the theoreticians and visionaries of modern India in the nineteenth century, was reformulated in terms of a certain creative reordering of the milieu at the level of symbolic action. Referring mainly to Tagore (as well as to contemporaries reacting to him) and Aurobindo, I argued that the presence of a clearly external, colonial authority made it urgent for the people in India to come to terms with their own wishes, aspirations and traditional aims, seeking a principle of harmony that would unify their efforts under a common purpose. The idea of Śakti (energy, will) that was invoked in this period is analogous to the concept of dynamic energy that is pivotal to

Freud's conceptual architecture. It has been suggested that all instances of human love in India, public as well as private, are related to the default view (and therefore the typical functioning) of the family in this country and to the place of the mother as it comes across and is registered in early, infantile, experience. Formulations that become accessible to the growing child and the adult obviously restructure it a great deal and enrich the protagonist's[3] understanding, but cannot completely replace the structure that reflects the basic settings of the culture. Those settings remain in the "family romance" genre, all the way to the end; if there was ever a place where the genre is robustly relevant, India is that place. The idea of love in this country did incorporate some elements of Western romanticism to the extent that intercultural blending proved possible; themes of children's wish fulfilment provided one site for such reception; another was India's highly-developed poetry of emotive devotionality and its associated music. The idea, prevalent in India, of cosmic energy as a feminine force, articulated in the tantric tradition and rooted in the systematic concept of *prakṛti* in Sāṁkhya doctrines, contributed to the texture of love as it evolved as a construct in successive formulations by the seminal thinkers of modern India.

The use of myths – which unleashed the evocative power of their key symbols in the past and renews their force differently in the context of recent interventions – has been discussed in Chapter 4. The impact of the mediaeval Bhakti movements, which fashioned new solutions to the riddles that love had to face in India, is another theme of this chapter. The spread and the renewed surge of *bhakti* in recent centuries presents a scene of what might be described as "the return of the repressed" in Freudian terms, but this return has occurred in India without the vehemence or open hostility that such a

[3] See fn. 1.

description would lead one to expect. The notion of a non-vehement return of the repressed, and a specific proposal crucially referring to the Indian landscape, are to be elaborated in the book based on this report. Some of the Freudian tenets which need to be reformulated in view of the present study will also be discussed there.[4]

The findings of this study make it plausible to suggest that the lack of initiative in forming and cultivating bonds of friendship (as well as the corresponding absence or paucity of such portrayals in contemporary literature) reflects the relative absence of openings or perceived opportunities for launching joint projects in the social structure as it has emerged.

I conclude this report by taking a leaf out of Anzieu's observation that in modern times, in spite of all the permissiveness in Western societies, man is not at ease with his body; I would like to make the analogous point that even after finding new ways to acquire money, power and pleasure, Indians are not more at ease with their bodies and souls than they had been under conditions of deprivation. Talking about love and friendship is yet to make them more loving or more friendly. Freud has helped me to look at them – or rather to look at *us*, I include myself as well, of course – with searching but understanding eyes.

---

[4] See fn. 2.

Index